My Financial Toolbox

The Nuts and Bolts of Managing Your Money

Harry Sit

To my father, who taught me the value of lifetime learning.

Contents

Contents

Contents

Acknowledgements

I'd like to thank readers of *The Finance Buff* blog. This book would not be possible without them.

Ashit Patel, Robert Kanterman, Stephen Abney, Oksana B., Daria Fedyukina, L. Dugent, V. Chandrasekhar, Stephen Wong, Will Hea, Tom Paluta, and 7 other readers reviewed a draft of this book and provided valuable comments and suggestions. Techno Peasant and Dave Gilmer proofread and corrected hundreds of typos and usage errors in a draft. Together, we donated $1,100 to The Salvation Army to support families in need.

My Financial Toolbox

The Nuts and Bolts of Managing
Your Money

Introduction

My wife and I are first-generation immigrants to the U.S. We came in our mid-20's for graduate school with only a few hundred dollars in our pockets. Being new to the country, we didn't know anything about the U.S. financial system. Before we arrived, we never had a checking account or a credit card. We never filled out any tax form. We were forced to learn everything.

My first job after graduate school was in the employee benefits department of a large unionized manufacturing company. It was my job to give the presentation to new hires about their benefits: health insurance, pension, 401(k), life insurance, disability insurance, flexible spending accounts, and so on. I had to learn from scratch because I never had any of those benefits myself. I took professional training and became a Certified Employee Benefits Specialist (CEBS).

As time went by, I came to realize that my having to learn from scratch was actually an advantage. Others who grew up with the system didn't necessarily know more about these topics because they didn't have the need to learn them systematically. I started sharing what I learned about personal finance and investing on my blog *The Finance Buff* (thefinancebuff.com) in 2006. Last year 1.9 million people visited my blog. When I mention to people that I write a blog about personal finance, some would ask me how I do this or that. I tell them and then the conversation moves on to another topic. They probably have more questions but they must think it's impolite to probe.

No problem. In this book I'll open up and share with you everything in my financial toolbox. When I say everything, I mean *everything*, from checking account to savings account, from credit cards to home mortgage, every type of insurance, and every investment account.

I explain what they are for, what features I look for in a good provider, which companies and what products I use, and why. Instead of saying generically that you should have an emergency fund, I tell you exactly where I put my emergency fund.

Who Should Read This Book

I'm assuming you already have a good handle on your income and spending. If you simply don't earn enough, your first priority should be to increase your income. If you're spending too much relative to your income, your first priority should be to lower your spending. Many other books already address the income, spending, and budgeting angles. I'm not repeating them here.

This book is about the nuts and bolts of managing your money. As in any other job, using good tools makes the job much easier, but tools in and of themselves don't change the fundamental nature of the job. Income and spending still come first. You should read this book if you'd like to learn how to make the most of your money when you're comfortable with your income and spending.

Not an Infomercial

Recommending financial products is a big business. Some websites that recommend bank accounts and credit cards have well over $100 million in venture capital funding. These sites exist to promote their advertisers. If the best product doesn't pay them well enough, it won't come up on top. Their interest is in having you open an account with one of their advertisers. It doesn't matter which one, as long as you use *their* link to open an account.

I used to have affiliate relationships too. If someone used a link on my website to apply for a credit card, I got paid a commission. I've withdrawn from all such relationships to avoid conflicts of interest.

None of the companies I mention in this book pay me for mentioning them.

"Good Enough" and "Set and Forget"

I use "good enough" and "set and forget" as two guiding principles in choosing which tools I use in my financial toolbox.

The 80/20 rule, also known as the Pareto Principle, says roughly 80% of the effects come from 20% of the causes. In personal finance, it's more like 95/5. 5% of the effort will get you 95% there. You can spend a lot more time and effort to chase the last 5%, and that last 5% still isn't guaranteed.

I also treat time as a precious property. If something requires constant caring and feeding, I'd rather direct my attention elsewhere and choose something else that "just works" after I set it up once.

I wrote this book from a consumer's point of view. I'm not a financial advisor, an attorney, or an accountant. I selected these tools to fit my own interest and use them to achieve my goals. Personal finance is *personal*. Naturally not everything I use will be the best for you. My goal with this book is to quickly get you to the 95% level with 5% of the effort.

Use this book as an exercise to review your financial toolbox. If your tools work better for you, great, keep them. If you see a better tool, consider replacing yours. If you see you're missing a tool, consider adding it to your financial toolbox. You'll improve how you manage your financial life.

Reminders

All product features, pricing, and interest rates are as of February 2020. They are subject to change by the providers outside my control. Please double-check the current features and pricing before you decide to use any of the tools mentioned in this book.

Tax laws are complex. I'm not able to cover all the nuances in this book. Please consult IRS publications, a tax professional, or an updated tax book for details.

Chapter 1 Everyday Banking and Spending

We start with the tools for everyday banking and spending. For most people, this toolset includes a checking account, a savings account, and a couple of credit cards.

Checking Account

A checking account serves as a hub. I use it for receiving deposits, withdrawing cash, writing checks, paying bills, and transfers between accounts.

I do my banking primarily online. A good checking account should have no monthly fee, no minimum balance requirement, fast crediting for deposits, and no fees for cash withdrawals. It's also important to have unlimited links to your other accounts and fast transfers when you move money between accounts.

Most checking accounts have the standard online and mobile banking features including free bill payments and mobile deposits. Some banks and credit unions don't have the option to link to external accounts. Some charge a fee for transferring money to external accounts. Those aren't acceptable. A better checking account has a large ATM network, reimburses ATM surcharges from other banks, processes transfers to and from outside accounts efficiently, and pays competitive interest on the balance.

Please remember none of the companies I mention in the book pay me anything for mentioning them.

Fidelity Cash Management Account

I use a Fidelity Cash Management Account as my primary checking account. Although technically, it's an investment account not a checking account, it's specifically designed to function as a traditional checking account.

You open the Cash Management Account with Fidelity Investments (fidelity.com). The account has no monthly fee, and it requires no minimum balance. The balance is FDIC insured, earning a 0.82% interest rate, which is higher than the rate you get on many other checking accounts (0.45% at Alliant Credit Union, see below; 0.10% at Ally Bank). For a $5,000 average balance in the account, Fidelity Cash Management pays you $41 in a year when Ally Bank pays you $5. Although the difference isn't much in dollars, getting a higher interest rate on your money gives you a feeling of fairness.

You get a routing number and an account number for direct deposit and auto pay, a free checkbook, a debit card that reimburses all ATM fees, free bill pay, and free mobile deposit. You can link your other accounts elsewhere to the Fidelity Cash Management Account. Free electronic funds transfers (also known as ACH transfers) to and from those other accounts are processed quickly. While some other banks take two or three business days to do a transfer, Fidelity takes only one business day. If you need even faster transfers, Fidelity will do wire transfers for free (some receiving banks charge a fee for incoming wires).

Having all ATM fees reimbursed is a game-changer if you never had it before. It means when you need cash, you can use any ATM you see. If the ATM charges a fee (both in the U.S. and international), Fidelity will reimburse it in a few days, and there is no cap on how much Fidelity will reimburse in a month. When you travel overseas, getting foreign currency through an ATM gives you the best exchange rate.

You can go fancier by buying a money market fund inside the Cash Management Account for a higher interest rate (see page 12), but that's optional. Just using the Cash Management Account as-is out of the box already makes it a great checking account. Fidelity can offer all these features in the Cash Management Account because Fidelity is an investment company. The Cash Management Account solidifies its relationship with customers for investing. It isn't necessarily a profit center in and of itself.

Fidelity Investments has branch offices in some cities. If you have a branch near you and you need to deposit a large check that you aren't comfortable depositing through the mobile phone, you can drop off the check for deposit at the branch office.

You can't deposit physical cash or get a cashier's check with a Fidelity Cash Management Account. I use a Bank of America checking account in the rare occasions when I need to deposit cash or get a cashier's check (see page 8).

Alliant Credit Union

Before I moved my primary checking account to the Fidelity Cash Management Account, I used a High-Interest Checking account at Alliant Credit Union.

A credit union is like a bank, but it's owned by its customers, who join and become members of the credit union. Profits go back to the members in the form of higher interest rates on deposits and lower interest rates on loans. Alliant Credit Union in Chicago serves members nationwide. It's the 7th largest credit union in the U.S. Anyone can join Alliant Credit Union by being a PTA member or by making a one-time $10 donation to a supported charity Foster Care to Success.

When you use Alliant Credit Union, you can do everything online and through ATMs. In all the years I used Alliant Credit Union, I'd never gone into a branch.

Alliant Credit Union's free checking account charges no monthly fee, with no minimum balance requirement. You get a free debit card, a free box of standard checks, free online banking with free bill payments, and free mobile deposits. If you have at least one electronic deposit per month and you opt-out of paper statements, you get paid 0.45% interest on your checking account balance.

You can add any number of external accounts for electronic transfers. Alliant Credit Union processes transfers very efficiently. If you make your request before a cutoff time, your outgoing transfer will arrive at the destination the following business day.

Alliant Credit Union makes it feel like a local bank by its large ATM network. Customers have access to 80,000 surcharge-free ATMs. By comparison, Bank of America has 18,000 ATMs in the country. Some ATMs available to Alliant Credit Union also take deposits of both cash and checks. These ATMs are marked as deposit-taking ATMs in the ATM Locator online and in their mobile app. If you have to withdraw cash from another bank's ATM, Alliant Credit Union reimburses up to $20 a month in ATM fees, although withdrawing cash outside the U.S. incurs a 1% fee. In the few times I had to call customer service, the U.S.-based reps were always friendly and helpful.

All these features make Alliant Credit Union a great choice for a checking account. Getting paid interest and having ATM surcharges reimbursed is better than other banks that pay no interest and have a limited number of ATMs. I moved away from Alliant Credit Union only because I have other accounts at Fidelity, and having everything together makes it easier to manage.

Bank of America

When you use a checking account from a place that has no local branches, on rare occasions you may still want local access, such as getting a cashier's check, depositing a check exceeding the limit for mobile deposit, depositing a large sum of cash that you don't feel comfortable feeding to an ATM, and access to free notary service or a safe deposit box at the bank branch. For those purposes, I keep a free checking account from Bank of America as a local backup.

A Bank of America checking account is required for Bank of America's Preferred Rewards program, which I'll go into later in this chapter (page 17). Under the Preferred Rewards program, the checking account is free, with no minimum balance requirement. It comes with a whole suite of features I don't really use because it's not my primary checking account. I usually keep no more than $100 in the Bank of America checking account.

Reward Checking Accounts

Some banks and credit unions offer reward checking accounts that pay a high interest rate up to a certain balance cap, typically $10,000 to $15,000, provided that you perform certain activities, which usually include using the debit card 10-15 times a month.

For example, Lake Michigan Credit Union in Grand Rapids, Michigan pays 3% interest on up to $15,000 in its Max Checking account if you:

- Have direct deposit;
- Receive e-statement;
- Make at least 10 debit card purchases per month; and
- Log in at least four times to online banking

A savings account usually pays a higher interest rate than a checking account. The 3% rate on this reward checking account is even higher than the rate on a typical savings account. The only thing is you'll have to jump through some hoops, and it's only on a balance up to the $15,000 cap. If you have a way to meet the requirements naturally, such as buying lunch every day at work with the debit card, it may be worth it, but if you have to keep track and count how many times you used the debit card this month or how many times you logged in to online banking, it will be a distraction.

If you don't find meeting the requirements difficult, you can consider using a reward checking account. Depositaccounts.com has listings of reward checking accounts from different banks and credit unions in the country. Some banks and credit unions let you open an account from anywhere. Some restrict the accounts to only local customers. I don't use a reward checking account because it's not "set and forget."

Short-Term Savings

You also need an account for saving toward a goal or as a reserve for unexpected expenses (an "emergency fund"). You keep this money in a savings account or a money market fund to separate the money from your day-to-day spending and to earn a higher interest than in a checking account.

A savings account is the simplest tool in your financial toolbox. You put money in, and it earns interest. If you need to tap your savings, it's easy to transfer some money out to your checking account.

Every bank or credit union offers a savings account. Deposits in a bank or credit union are insured by the government agency FDIC or NCUA for up to $250,000 per account holder. A good savings account should have no monthly fee, no minimum balance requirement, and a high interest rate.

Online Savings Account

You can have a savings account at the same place as your checking account. The interest rate may not be the highest but that makes transfers between your checking account and your savings account instant.

If you open a savings account elsewhere, you can potentially get a higher interest rate. For example, the interest rate on the High-Rate Savings account at Alliant Credit Union is 1.6%, while the interest rate on the savings account at BrioDirect is 2.05%. Because BrioDirect doesn't offer a checking account, a transfer between your checking account and BrioDirect savings account takes at least one business day.

Federal Reserve regulations ("Regulation D") limit the number of online and pre-scheduled withdrawals from a savings account to no more than six times a month. Keep this limit in mind when you transfer out of your savings account. There are no limits on how many times you can transfer *into* a savings account.

You can look up which bank or credit union is offering the highest rate right now on depositaccounts.com, but keep in mind that banks and credit unions change their rates constantly. Rather than choosing the one offering the highest rate today, you're better off going with an institution that consistently offers a competitive rate. They don't necessarily have the highest rate at any moment, but they don't give you a poor rate either. They fit my principles of "good enough" and "set and forget."

The following banks have offered competitive rates consistently in recent years. I include the current interest rate on their savings accounts for reference. The rates change frequently.

- CIT Bank (1.8%)
- Synchrony Bank (1.7%)
- Marcus by Goldman Sachs (1.7%)
- Discover Bank (1.6%)
- Alliant Credit Union (1.6%)
- Ally Bank (1.6%)

Money Market Fund

A money market fund is an investment product offered by a mutual fund company. Although government agencies don't insure money market funds, they do require the funds must invest only in safe and very short-term investments.

To a customer, a money market fund works just like a savings account: you put money in it, you earn interest at the end of the month, and you can withdraw from it at any time. Unlike a savings account, there are no limits on the number of times you can withdraw from a money market fund in a month.

The amount of interest you can earn from a money market fund can be slightly higher or slightly lower than the interest you get from an online savings account. Yields on money market funds change daily with the market. For comparison, here are the current yields of a few good money market funds:

- Vanguard Prime Money Market Fund (VMMXX) – 1.64%
- Schwab Value Advantage Money Fund (SWVXX) – 1.49%
- Fidelity Money Market Fund (SPRXX) – 1.44%

There are several types of money market funds. They differ primarily by what they invest in and how the dividends are taxed. A prime money market fund invests in instruments issued by both government and corporate entities. It typically has a slightly higher yield. A government or treasury money market fund invests in only instruments issued by government entities. It typically has a slightly lower yield but the amount you earn may be fully or partially exempt from state income tax. A municipal ("muni") money market fund invests in instruments issued by state and city government entities. Its yield is exempt from federal income tax. The yield on a state-specific municipal money market fund is exempt from both federal income tax and state income tax of that state.

The money market fund's type, its yield, and your tax bracket will determine which fund ends up with the highest yield after taxes.

If you'd like to figure it out, you can use a calculator on my blog (see Appendix), but don't fret it. Just picking one and sticking with it will be "good enough." While you can switch freely between funds, it's not worth the attention load. You have bigger fish to fry!

Because I use a Fidelity Cash Management Account as my primary checking account, I buy a money market fund inside that account to make it a checking-savings combo. When I have too much money in the checking part, I put the excess into the money market fund. When I'm short in checking, I sell from the money market fund. If I forget, Fidelity will automatically sell from the money market fund to cover any shortfall. Although I can get a higher interest rate if I use an online savings account elsewhere, this is "good enough" for me.

When I used Alliant Credit Union for my primary checking account, I also used its savings account for my emergency fund. When I had more money than I needed in the checking account, I transferred into the savings account. When I needed more money in the checking account, I transferred from the savings account. All transfers between the checking account and the savings account happened instantly. Having both checking and savings accounts at the same place makes it convenient.

Some people may prefer a distance between their checking account and their savings account to reduce the temptation to spend the money in their savings account. That works too. If you decide to keep your savings account at a different place than your checking account, whenever you transfer funds between two accounts, if possible, always initiate it from the sending account (a "push"). When you transfer from checking to savings, initiate it from the institution that has your checking account. When transferring from savings to checking, initiate it from the institution that has your savings account.

When you do a "push" the sending bank knows you have enough money for the transfer and the receiving bank won't place a hold on the incoming money. If you initiate the transfer from the receiving account (a "pull") the receiving bank doesn't know whether you have enough money at the source. It can place a hold on the money pulled in.

Fintech Products

Some financial technology ("fintech") startup companies also offer accounts with checking or savings features. Because they have funding from venture capital, they can afford to offer an attractive rate, at least when their products are still new, to build up a customer base.

For example, fintech companies Wealthfront, Betterment, Robinhood, and SoFi all offer a cash management account with features similar to a checking account and a savings account. The interest rates on the accounts are competitive with rates on an online savings account or money market fund. If you happen to use these companies for investing (see Robo Advisors on page 131), it's convenient to have your checking account and savings account at the same place.

I still favor traditional companies with proven business models. I want my checking account and savings account to be boring and "just work." If you don't already use these fintech companies for investing, I don't see a compelling reason to use them just for checking and savings.

Credit Cards

I have a few credit cards. I use them for convenience and cash-back rewards, and I pay them in full every month.

It goes without saying if you don't pay in full every month, you shouldn't use a credit card. A debit card or a prepaid card would be better if you're not sure you can always pay in full. Not earning rewards is much better than paying 19% interest on credit card balances.

Don't pat yourself on the back if you pay in full every month. Fully one half to 2/3 of all cardholders do. The percentage is probably even greater in higher income households. It's not that unusual, and banks are well aware of it. They create the impression that you're making money off of them to make you use their cards. Banks still make money on your purchases from the fees they charge the merchants. The merchants factor the fees they pay to the banks in the prices they charge you. In the end you're still paying the banks' fees through the prices you pay to the merchants.

However, because banks made lawmakers prohibit merchants from imposing surcharges on using a credit card, at most places the prices you pay are the same no matter how you pay. You won't get the products for less if you don't use a credit card. Since you're paying the higher prices with the credit card fees already factored in, you'll at least earn some rewards when you use a credit card for purchases.

Some gas stations offer discounts if you pay with a debit card. Some utilities offer a discount if you pay with a debit card or a bank account. Some places charge a fee for using a credit card. Those are the exceptions. I use a credit card for purchases everywhere else.

In addition to earning rewards and making back some of the fees you pay, using a credit card gives you better protection from unauthorized charges than using a debit card. When you have unauthorized charges on a credit card, the bill isn't due yet. During the time it takes for the bank to reverse the charges, you can continue using the card or use a different card. When you have unauthorized charges on a debit card, the money has already left your checking account. If the bank doesn't credit you back promptly, other checks or autopay's may bounce. Although eventually you'll be made whole, having unauthorized charges on a debit card causes chaos in your checking account.

Churning Cards vs Using Cards

There are two camps when it comes to getting rewards from credit cards: churning cards and using cards.

One camp gets rewards from the sign-up bonus. Credit cards usually offer a sign-up bonus with a requirement to spend a minimum amount within a set time. For example, a credit card offers 60,000 reward points if you spend at least $4,000 in the first three months. The 60,000 reward points can be worth $750. If you're in the "churning cards" camp, after you get the card and fulfill the spending requirement, you stop using that card and move on to applying for a different card and fulfilling the new spending requirement. If the previous card has an annual fee, you would close it before the next annual fee kicks in. Repeating this pattern over and over affects your credit score to some extent, but not bad enough to make you not qualify for the best rates on loans (see page 23).

You get more rewards this way, but it also requires more attention and tracking. You have to watch your spending on the card closely to make sure you hit the required spending level within the required period. If you don't normally spend that much per month, you'll have to find some creative ways to do some "manufactured spending," such as buying gift cards.

People in the "using cards" camp find the best cards for their normal spending patterns and use them. There is no pressure to spend a set amount within a set time or look for the next sign-up bonus, and no reason to close cards.

I belong to this second camp of "using cards" simply because I go by my principles of "good enough" and "set and forget." I spend my time and attention elsewhere. Other people who don't mind spending their time and attention do well in playing the card churning game.

Bank of America Preferred Rewards Program

I use credit cards in the Bank of America Preferred Rewards program. The Preferred Rewards program encourages customers to use Bank of America as a one-stop shop for banking, credit cards, and investing. You enroll in the Preferred Rewards program when you have:

- a Bank of America checking account;
- one or more Bank of America credit cards; and
- an investment account with Merrill Edge (owned by Bank of America)

When your combined balances in your Bank of America and Merrill Edge accounts are above $20,000, $50,000, or $100,000, you qualify for different tiers of benefits. For example, when you have $100,000 in combined balances, your Bank of America credit card rewards are boosted by 75%. When your credit card normally gives 1.5% reward for every purchase, the 75% boost adds 1.125% and makes the reward 2.625% for every purchase.

Combined Balances	Reward Boost	1.5% reward after boost
< $20,000	0%	1.5%
$20,000	25%	1.875%
$50,000	50%	2.25%
$100,000	75%	2.625%

Before you think it's crazy to keep $20,000, $50,000, or $100,000 idle cash in a bank account earning nearly nothing just for credit card rewards, please note the key to qualify for the bonus tiers is to use the value of your investments in a Merrill Edge account. You reach the bonus tier by transferring an IRA or an investment account to Merrill Edge. The transfer can be "in kind," which means you don't have to sell your investments in your previous account. Your Merrill

Edge account will receive and hold the same investments as before. The value of those investments will now count toward your qualification for credit card reward bonus.

You don't need a Bank of America branch near you to open Bank of America accounts. The checking account, credit cards, and the Merrill Edge account can all be opened easily online. You don't have to use the Bank of America checking account as your primary checking account. Keeping only a small balance works. I usually keep less than $100 in my Bank of America checking account.

You don't have to use the Merrill Edge account for investing either. Holding some investments there for the long-term will do. After I transferred an account to Merrill Edge several years ago, I haven't made any transactions in my Merrill Edge account. The investments are just sitting there and growing with automatic dividend reinvestments. My Bank of America checking account and Merrill Edge account are there only to qualify for the Preferred Rewards program for the higher rewards on Bank of America credit cards.

If you do use the Merrill Edge account for investing, it charges zero account maintenance fee and zero commission for ETFs (see page 127).

Bank of America Cash Rewards Card

I use a Bank of America Cash Rewards card for online shopping, as it has no annual fee and it lets you designate one special category for 3% rewards. I chose *online shopping* as my designated category because I make many purchases online these days. The other possible special categories are gas, dining, drug stores, home improvement, and travel.

Combined Balances	Reward Boost	3% reward after boost
< $20,000	0%	3%
$20,000	25%	3.75%
$50,000	50%	4.5%
$100,000	75%	5.25%

The Cash Rewards card has a 3% foreign transaction fee. If you choose travel as your special category, keep in mind that buying tickets from many international airlines will count as a foreign transaction even though the tickets are priced in U.S. dollars.

It's possible to change the designated category monthly as your spending patterns change, but I set it permanently to online shopping (remember "set and forget"). The special category rewards are limited to $2,500 of spending in any calendar quarter. Because I don't spend that much in a quarter anyway, I don't track how close I'm getting to the cap. If you routinely spend more than $2,500 per quarter in the special category or if you wish to have another special category for the 3% rewards, you can get another flavor of the Cash Rewards card offered by Bank of America, such as a Susan G. Komen Cash Rewards card, an MLB card, a World Wildlife Fund card, or a U.S. Pride card. I don't bother with a second card that I have to remember for another special category. Only one card is "good enough" for me.

The cash-back rewards from the Cash Rewards card can be set in online banking to automatically redeem as a statement credit at the end of each month. That's another "set and forget."

Bank of America Travel Rewards Card

I use a Bank of America Travel Rewards card for everything else. This card has no annual fee and no foreign transaction fee. It pairs very well with the Bank of America Cash Rewards card. Together, these two cards make it simple in terms of figuring out which card to use where.

The Travel Rewards card pays 1.5% rewards when the rewards are redeemed against a travel charge. With a 50% boost from having $50,000 in the Preferred Rewards program, the 1.5% rewards become 2.25% rewards on every purchase. With a 75% boost from having $100,000 in the Preferred Rewards program, the 1.5% rewards become 2.625% rewards on every purchase.

The rewards have the best value when you redeem them for a credit on your statement against a travel charge. Travel includes airline, hotel, rental car, taxi (including Uber & Lyft), public transit, museum entrance, and ski passes. For example, if you had a $100 charge from a hotel within the last 12 months, you can redeem $100 worth of reward points for a $100 credit on your next statement. When you use this card for everything except the special category you reserve for the Cash Rewards card, naturally you'll hit some expenses in those travel categories. That will allow you to redeem your reward points.

With these two cards in the Bank of America Preferred Rewards program, you'll earn:

- up to 5.25% rewards on purchases in one special category from Bank of America Cash Rewards card; and
- up to 2.625% rewards on everything else from Bank of America Travel Rewards card

It's very easy to remember and manage.

Bank of America Premium Rewards Card

Bank of America also has a Premium Rewards card. It's similar to the Travel Rewards card, except it has a $95 annual fee. It also offers $100 in credits for ancillary airline charges (baggage fees, seat upgrades, etc.), and it gives a higher reward on travel and dining charges (2% versus 1.5% before Preferred Rewards bonus). If you charge a lot of travel and dining expenses or pay airline baggage fees, you can make it worth the $95 annual fee.

The rewards from the Premium Rewards card can also be set in online banking to automatically redeem as a statement credit at the end of each month.

Auto Pay

I have all my bills on auto pay. If a bill can be charged to a credit card without a fee, such as my cell phone bill and my auto insurance bill, I let them charge my credit card. If a bill can't be charged to a credit card or if there's a fee for charging to a credit card, such as my water bill and my electricity bill, I let them automatically debit my checking account. Automatic debits also pay my credit cards and car loan from my checking account. Before I paid off my mortgage, my mortgage payments were also on auto pay. If the person I'm paying can't automatically charge a credit card or debit a checking account, such as my gardener, I use the bank's bill pay system to pay them on a fixed schedule.

When everything is on auto pay, I don't have to remember to pay any bill manually. I can be out of the country for five months and all my bills will still be paid on time. I only need to make sure I have enough money in my checking account. When my checking account is a checking-savings combo with automatic overdraft transfers from savings to checking, as in the Fidelity Cash Management account, I only need to make sure I have enough money in the combo.

Some people worry about giving out their checking account routing number and account number for auto pay. They worry that the billers would debit twice or debit the wrong amount. Although it can happen theoretically, it never happened to me in my 20 years of using the auto pay setup. I think the chance of missing a payment when you do it manually is much higher. Even though you can often have the late fee waived, it's still a hassle. The convenience and peace of mind in using auto pay outweigh any theoretical hiccups.

Auto Pay for Bank of America Credit Cards

Setting up auto pay of the full statement balance for Bank of America credit cards isn't very intuitive. If you decide to use Bank of America credit cards, I have a walkthrough on my blog for how to set up auto pay for the full statement balance (see Appendix). Fortunately, you only do it once since after that the system will automatically debit the full statement balance every month from your primary checking account.

Chapter 2 Loans

While I try to pay for consumer purchases with my own money, sometimes loans are still useful. When the interest rate is favorable, it can be smarter to get a loan than paying cash. If you don't let the availability of loans influence your purchasing decision, a loan is just another tool. First, you decide whether to make the purchase. Then you decide how you'll pay for it – with your own money or with a loan.

Credit Score

Your credit score affects the interest rate you'll get on a loan. Your credit score only has to be "very good" for you to qualify for the best interest rate. Improving an already good credit score doesn't make any difference.

Credit bureaus such as Experian, Equifax, and TransUnion collect data from companies on your credit balances and your payment history. Fair Isaac Corporation (FICO) develops algorithms that distill these data into a numeric score for different usage. FICO licenses its algorithms to the credit bureaus, which then report your credit scores to the current and prospective lenders.

According to FICO, as of September 2019, 43% of the U.S. population has a FICO score of 750 or above. Scores 750-799 are considered "very good" and scores 800-850 are considered "excellent." Lenders usually give their best interest rate to borrowers with a FICO score above 740. When you already qualify for the best interest rate, it doesn't matter whether your score is 770 or 840. If you simply use credit when you need it, and pay back as promised, you'll have a very good credit score, and you'll qualify for the best interest rate when you need to borrow.

I don't check my credit score often, but when I need it, I get it free from online banking at Bank of America. Bank of America provides a FICO score based on credit report data from TransUnion. Because I placed a security freeze on my credit (see page 32), I don't need a credit monitoring service such as Credit Karma. If you'd like to check for errors in your credit reports, you can get one from each credit bureau once a year at annualcreditreport.com.

Auto Loan

When you buy a new car, the manufacturer often offers 0% APR financing. When you can choose either 0% APR financing or an extra rebate, you're usually better off paying cash and pocketing the extra rebate. When you don't get any extra rebate if you decline the manufacturer's 0% APR financing, it makes sense to take the 0% APR financing and keep your money in a savings account. That was the case when I bought a car two years ago. I could pay cash but I chose the 0% APR financing for 60 months.

Sometimes the manufacturer offers an extra rebate if you take their financing (not 0% APR). You can take the financing, get the rebate, and then pay off the loan after a month. Auto loans typically don't have any prepayment penalty. A month's worth of interest is much less than the rebate.

Outside these special cases, you're better off buying a car with cash. It makes the buying process easy. If you already have a car loan, and the rate isn't 0%, you should pay it off. When you compare the interest rate on a car loan with the interest rate on a savings account, be sure to consider taxes. A 1.9% APR car loan costs more than a 1.9% savings account, because you pay taxes on the interest you earn in a savings account. If your savings account pays 1.9% interest and your tax rate is 30%, after taxes you're only getting 1.9% * 70% = 1.26%. The interest you pay on the car loan isn't tax deductible. After taxes, it doesn't make sense to earn 1.26% on your savings and pay 1.9% on your car loan. In the current low-interest environment, paying off a loan beats keeping money in a savings account.

Student Loan

While the prevailing sentiment is very much against student loans, I don't think it's the student loans' fault. If you have a heavy burden of student loans, blame the university that charged you a high tuition. If the degree is worth the tuition, it's still worth it even if you paid with student loans. If the degree isn't worth the tuition, it's still not worth it even if you had the money and paid cash.

Public Service Loan Forgiveness

If you work for a government or a not-for-profit organization, you may be able to receive loan forgiveness under the federal Public Service Loan Forgiveness program. It only works for *Direct Loans* after you have made 120 *qualifying* monthly payments under a *qualifying* repayment plan while working full-time for a *qualifying* employer. The loan type and the three "qualifying" keywords are very important. You must make sure your loan, your payments, your repayment plan, and your employer all meet the requirements for possible forgiveness.

All loans from the federal government after July 2010 were Direct Loans. Some federal loans made before that time were guaranteed by the federal government, but they weren't Direct Loans. If your federal loan isn't a Direct Loan, it's possible to consolidate it into a Direct Loan and make it eligible for forgiveness, but only payments after it turned into a Direct Loan will count as qualifying payments. Private loans from banks, not from the federal government, don't qualify for the forgiveness program.

Qualifying payments have their own set of requirements. Late payments don't count. Voluntary payments when you aren't required to pay because you're in school or because you're in a grace period, deferment, or forbearance don't count. Prepayments carried over from a previous month don't count.

You must enroll in an income-driven repayment plan, which comes in four flavors with confusing names and nuances for each:

- Revised Pay As You Earn Repayment Plan (REPAYE)
- Pay As You Earn Repayment Plan (PAYE)
- Income-Based Repayment Plan (IBR)
- Income-Contingent Repayment Plan (ICR)

Only the months you work full-time for a government or a non-profit organization count. You have to have someone at your employer sign an Employment Certification form annually or when you change jobs. If you don't work full-time for a government or a non-profit organization for at least 120 months, you won't qualify even if you meet all other requirements.

Finally, only the amount above what you already paid off after making 120 qualifying payments in a qualifying repayment plan is forgiven. It's possible after 10 years of payments, not much will be left.

If you're aiming to have part of your student loan forgiven under the Public Service Loan Forgiveness program, be sure to follow *all* the rules and keep meticulous records of your payments to show you're meeting all the requirements.

Pay Off ASAP

If you don't qualify for the Public Service Loan Forgiveness program because you don't work for a government or a non-profit organization, ideally you didn't borrow too much in student loans relative to your income. When you already have student loans, I believe the best way to handle them is to pay them off as soon as possible.

Depending on your income, the student loan interest may be tax deductible up to $2,500 per year. In 2020, the eligibility to deduct the student loan interest starts to phase out when your modified adjusted gross income (MAGI) reaches $70,000 for singles or $140,000 for married filing jointly. For most people, your MAGI for this purpose is your adjusted gross income (AGI) before subtracting any deduction for student loan interest. If you're paying more than $2,500 per year in student loan interest, the amount above $2,500 per year isn't tax deductible regardless of your income.

Regardless of whether you can deduct the student loan interest, chances are the student loan interest rates are still much higher than the returns you can earn on safe investments. Paying off the student loan is a great investment with guaranteed returns.

Refinance Student Loans

While you aggressively pay off the student loans, you can also try to refinance the loans to a lower interest rate. When you refinance, you borrow a new loan to pay off the existing loans. You'll be able to pay off the new loan faster when it has a lower interest rate.

Many companies offer student loan refinancing. These companies typically don't charge any application or origination fees. While the federal loans are fixed-rate loans, you can choose either a fixed rate or a variable rate for the refinanced loan. Because the refinanced loan will be a private loan, it doesn't have the income-driven repayment plans for federal loans. For more information on some of the student loan refinance programs, please go to this link:

www.whitecoatinvestor.com/student-loan-refinancing

Home Mortgage

When I had a home mortgage, I started with a 30-year fixed-rate mortgage at 6%. After I refinanced it several times, it became a 15-year mortgage at a 2.5% fixed rate.

15-Year Fixed-Rate Mortgage

I believe a 15-year fixed-rate mortgage strikes the best balance between a lower rate and the peace of mind in having a fixed rate. The two major decisions on selecting the type of mortgage are:

- fixed-rate or adjustable-rate; and
- 15-year or 30-year term

A fixed-rate mortgage offers a guarantee that the rate won't go up. If the prevailing rate in the market goes lower, you can refinance. An adjustable-rate mortgage (ARM) offers a fixed rate in the first few years but the rate can go up or down following a rate index afterward. ARMs typically have a 30-year term. A 15-year fixed-rate mortgage has a lower rate than the 30-year fixed-rate mortgage because the lender is taking less risk.

For example, here are the rates I saw for different types of mortgage with a similar closing cost:

- 30-year fixed-rate: 3.5%
- 5/1 ARM: 3.75%
- 15-year fixed-rate: 3.0%

ARMs are indicated by two numbers, for example a 5/1 ARM, a 7/1 ARM, or a 5/5 ARM. The first number shows the number of years the rate is fixed. The second number shows how frequently the rate will adjust after the initial fixed-rate period. A 5/1 ARM has the rate fixed for five years and the rate will adjust every year afterward.

Here the ARM has the highest rate in the first five years because the market expects the rate will go down afterward. That expectation may or may not materialize. In previous years a 5/1 ARM had a lower rate in the first 5 years, with an expectation of higher rates afterward. When the initial rate in an ARM is lower, you should consider how much higher the rate can go, whether you'll still be able to afford the payments if the rate goes up, and how long you'll stay in this home. With a 15-year fixed-rate mortgage, it's comforting to know you'll have a lower rate fixed for the full 15 years.

The only downside in a 15-year fixed-rate mortgage is that you have a higher required monthly payment. The required payments for a $400,000 loan at the rates above are:

- 30-year fixed-rate at 3.5%: $1,796/month
- 5/1 ARM at 3.75%: $1,852/month
- 15-year fixed at 3.0%: $2,762/month

The higher monthly payments force you to buy a smaller home than you otherwise could. If you can't afford the monthly payments on a 15-year mortgage, maybe the home is too expensive for you.

Some people think they can take the 30-year mortgage for lower monthly payments and invest the difference for a higher return. While this may work out in the very long term, it takes a long time to break even, because the interest rate on the entire loan is higher in a 30-year mortgage.

In our example here, the 0.5% higher rate on a $400,000 loan costs $2,000 more in interest in the first year, while investing the $966/month difference in monthly payments at a return of 5% per year will only earn a little over $200 in the first year. After 15 years, the extra interest you paid still exceeds the total investments you accumulate. Even if you're able to earn 8% on your investments, it still takes 8 years to catch up to the 0.5% higher interest paid on the loan. Besides, while the lower interest rate on a 15-year mortgage is guaranteed, an 8% investment return is not.

Refinance

If you already have a mortgage, you can consider refinancing it to a 15-year fixed-rate loan. When you refinance, you borrow a new loan to pay off the old loan. Most home mortgages don't have any prepayment penalty.

One concern is that when you refinance, you'll reset the clock on the mortgage. If you're three years into a 15-year mortgage, refinancing will extend the payoff date to 15 years from now as opposed to 12 years. It doesn't have to be that way. If you're lowering the interest rate by refinancing your loan, and you make the same monthly payment as before, which is higher than the new required monthly payment, the extra principal payments will pay off the loan before the original payoff date.

Another concern about refinancing is the closing cost. The closing cost includes costs for appraisal, title insurance, government recording fees, and processing fees charged by the escrow agents. It's a real concern for a small loan (less than $100,000) but not necessarily for a larger loan. If you pay the closing cost, you'll have to stay in the loan long enough for the savings from the lower rate to cover the closing cost. On a small loan, when the closing cost is high relative to the loan balance, that breakeven period can be very long.

Many banks offer "no-cost" refinances on larger loans. The bank will cover the closing cost in exchange for a slightly higher interest rate. As long as the slightly higher no-cost rate is still lower than the current interest rate on your loan, you benefit from refinancing from day one. It takes the uncertainty out of refinancing.

My favorite place for refinancing a mortgage is First Internet Bank of Indiana (www.firstib.com, "FirstIB"). FirstIB is a bank in Indianapolis. The loan officers there use the phone, email, and the Internet to originate loans.

You get clear quotes for the interest rate and the closing cost on their website without having to submit any personal information.

When the quoted lender credit covers the closing cost, it's a "no-cost" refinance. You apply online and submit all documents to a secure site online. The loan officer will arrange for an appraisal. When it comes to closing, they'll send a notary to your home or office to collect your signatures. After the loan is done, it's quickly transferred to a major bank for servicing.

When I had a mortgage, I refinanced several times with FirstIB. I always got what I was quoted. There were no gotcha's or surprises. My refinanced loans were transferred to Citi or Chase afterward for servicing. The transfer and servicing were all very smooth.

Prepaying Mortgage

Making an extra payment toward the principal of the mortgage earns a guaranteed return at the interest rate on the mortgage. Most home mortgages don't have any prepayment penalty. For example, if you have a 15-year fixed-rate mortgage at 3%, paying $10,000 extra toward the principal of this mortgage will lower the interest charged by $300 each year. This gives you a guaranteed return of 3% per year.

Moreover, this return is often a tax-free return because 95% of all taxpayers take the standard deduction now. Paying $300 more in mortgage interest doesn't give them any extra tax deduction. A 3% guaranteed tax-free return can compare favorably with buying muni bonds or other fixed-income investments. If you're satisfied with this level of return, it's worth considering prepaying your mortgage.

However, you lose the liquidity for the money used to prepay the mortgage. If you need to get the money out, you'll have to sell the home, refinance (possibly to a higher rate), or take another loan against the home, all of which can add unwanted costs to the transaction. Therefore, you should be sure you have plenty of liquidity from other sources before you prepay your mortgage. If the interest rate on your mortgage is higher than the current market rate on a 15-year fixed-rate mortgage, consider refinancing the mortgage to a 15-year fixed-rate first.

I paid off my mortgage early, but it was low on my list. I did it only after I had plenty of other investments.

Credit Freeze

Because I'm all set with credit cards and loans I want, I froze my credit with all three major credit bureaus to prevent identity thieves from opening new credit in my name. When your credit is frozen, a lender won't be able to check your credit using your Social Security Number. After you freeze your credit, you have an account and a password or a PIN to unfreeze your credit when needed. If you need a loan, you can temporarily unfreeze your credit and let the lender check your credit before you put it back on freeze again.

A law passed in 2018 made it free for anyone to freeze or unfreeze their credit at any time. You have to do it separately with each credit bureau. If you're married, each spouse has to place the freeze separately. To find the websites for freezing your credit, Google the name of the three major credit bureaus (Experian, Equifax, and TransUnion) together with the word "freeze." Each credit bureau has a separate account and password or PIN for each person for freezing and unfreezing. Note these passwords and PINs and save them securely (see page 158).

Some credit bureaus also offer a "credit lock" feature, which serves a similar purpose as a credit freeze. The difference is that your rights and the credit bureau's obligations in a credit freeze are mandated by law, whereas what the credit bureaus can or can't do with a credit lock are entirely up to the credit bureaus themselves. If they decide to do something when you have a credit lock enabled, they sure can, whereas if you have the credit freeze, their hands are tied by the law. Go for the official credit freeze, not the private credit lock.

ChexSystems

While you're at it, you can also place a security freeze with ChexSystems by Googling "ChexSystems freeze."

Many banks and credit unions check with ChexSystems when they receive an application for a new bank account. If you have a security freeze with ChexSystems, identity thieves won't be able to open bank accounts in your name at those banks and credit unions. When you need to open a new bank account yourself, you can temporarily unfreeze with ChexSystems and freeze again when you're done. Freezing and unfreezing with ChexSystems is also free.

Chapter 3 Insurance

We face many types of risks. Insurance mitigates the financial impact of these risks when the unexpected happens.

Life Insurance

Life insurance is for protecting your family from losing a source of income. If you die, you want your family to have enough money to continue their life journey. How much life insurance you need depends on how much your income is contributing to their financial well-being, how long they'll need it, and what other resources they have in case you die. Five to ten times your salary is a common guideline. Most people have their life insurance last through the year their youngest child graduates college.

When I had life insurance, I had the free life insurance offered by my employer, plus a term life policy I bought on my own. I no longer have life insurance now because my family already has sufficient financial resources in case I die.

Through Your Employer

All the companies I worked for offered basic life insurance to employees at two times their base pay. Your employer may offer similar coverage. It's free, but you have to pay taxes on the value of the employer-paid life insurance above $50,000. If you have young kids, two times your base pay probably isn't enough. You can buy additional life insurance through your employer's group policy, but you're better off buying it on your own.

Life insurance through an employer is usually "guaranteed issue," which means the insurance company accepts every new hire regardless of their health. Even if you have chronic health conditions, you can still sign up when you join a new employer. As a result, the premium rates the insurance company sets on the group policy aren't very attractive to healthy employees.

You may also lose the insurance if you leave your employer. Some group policies allow you to continue coverage by converting it to an individual policy. Again, the premium rates on the converted policy usually aren't attractive because only people who can't get coverage elsewhere tend to convert.

The premium rates on an employer group policy also usually increase with age. For example, here are the annual premiums for a $500,000 policy offered through one large employer for employees in different age groups:

Age	Non-Smokers	Smokers
< 30	$66	$144
30 - 34	$144	$156
35 - 39	$174	$192
40 - 44	$252	$294
45 - 49	$432	$504
50 - 54	$714	$834
55 - 59	$1,110	$1,308

As your age enters the next band, your premium will increase, whereas if you buy term life insurance on your own, you can get policies with guaranteed premiums that don't change for 15, 20, or 30 years. Therefore, even when the current premium on an employer group policy is comparable with the premium on a policy you can buy elsewhere, the employer group policy will become more expensive in later years.

Take the free policy offered by your employer and buy additional coverage independently elsewhere. This also applies to life insurance on your spouse offered through your employer. Unless your spouse is unable to get insurance elsewhere, buy it on your own. It doesn't make sense to buy life insurance on your children because your children don't earn an income.

Your employer may also offer you and/or your spouse Accidental Death & Dismemberment (AD&D) insurance. AD&D pays if you die or if you lose an eye or a limb, but it has to be due to an accident. Again, if it's free accept it, but don't buy any extra. You want coverage for your death or disability due to any reason, not just due to an accident. Save the money to buy term life insurance on your own.

Term Life Insurance

The best life insurance is *term life insurance*. It covers you for a set term: 10 years, 15 years, 20 years, 30 years, etc. You pick an amount and how long you want to be covered for. If you die within the term, the insurance company pays that amount to the designated beneficiaries. It's that simple.

The most popular term life policies are *level-premium* term life policies. In a level-premium policy, the annual premium stays the same throughout the policy's term. You pay that same amount year after year. Because the risk of death increases with age, in a level-premium policy you pay a little more than the true risk would dictate in early years and you pay a little less than the true risk in later years.

Another setup is an *annually renewable* term life policy, sometimes also called a *yearly renewable* term life policy. In this type of term policy, the premium increases each year, reflecting the increasing risk of death.

Either a level-premium term life policy or an annually renewable term life policy will work. Because more companies quote level-premium term life policies, level-premium term life policies are more competitive. Use competition among insurance companies to your advantage. However, if you only need a policy for a few years, an annually renewable term life policy can be better.

The best place to get term life insurance quotes is term4sale.com. This website doesn't sell insurance directly. You can check rates without disclosing any personally identifiable information. You choose the length of the term, the coverage amount, and the minimum rating of the insurance companies you're willing to consider.

The rating of an insurance company shows the financial strength of the insurance company. You want to make sure the insurance company is still in business and it's able to pay the claim if you die. AM Best is a widely used insurance rating company. I set the minimum rating I would consider to A+ by AM Best.

Life insurance rates differ by your health and any sports activities you engage that insurance companies consider as risky (for example, SCUBA diving or rock climbing). Insurance companies put you into a rating class depending on their evaluation of your risk of dying. You won't know what rating class you'll qualify for until the insurance company puts you through a medical exam. I would check the rates with different rating classes (Preferred Plus, Preferred, etc.) and see which few companies offer the lowest premiums.

For example, here are the annual premiums I got on a $1 million 20-year level-premium term life policy for a 32-year-old non-smoking female in my zip code, from companies with a minimum AM Best rating of A+:

Company	Preferred Plus	Preferred
Thrivent	$315	$425
Lincoln National Life	$316	$409
Banner Life	$317	$405
Protective Life	$322	$410

These rates are guaranteed to not change for the full 20-year term. As you can see, the premium quotes are within a narrow range among the top few companies. Which rating class you're placed in makes a bigger difference.

After you get a feel of the premium rates, you can get names of insurance agents from term4sale.com. You don't pay any more when you buy a term life insurance policy through an agent. The agent's commission is built into the price of the policy. If you have a few companies in mind, the agent may be able to tell you which company is more likely to accept you into a better rating class based on your specific health conditions or sports activities.

After you apply for term life insurance, the insurance company will send a nurse to your home or office to give you a free medical exam. The nurse will complete a health questionnaire with you, measure your height, weight, heart rate, blood pressure, and collect your blood and urine samples. If the company is satisfied with the exam results, you'll soon get your policy through your agent.

Usually, it's better to pay your term life insurance policy premium annually in one payment. Some companies will charge an administrative fee if you choose to pay monthly. Save the fee and pay annually.

Whole Life, Universal Life, VUL, IUL

Some insurance agents trying to earn a fat commission are the masters of creating confusion. They put out all kinds of obfuscation and redirection to argue for whole life, universal life, variable universal life (VUL), indexed universal life (IUL), or any other combination of mental gymnastics. If an insurance agent is trying to sell you anything except term life insurance, the simple answer is to say no and stop engaging in any further conversation.

Those products may be good for someone who has more money than they can ever use themselves. Chances are that someone isn't you. Just play dumb and don't bother debating with the insurance agent. The more time you spend on engaging with the insurance salesperson, the more time you'll waste. Worse yet is the regret if you succumb to the sales tactics. Those insurance agents are trained well to play up the benefits of the policies and play down the shortcomings. You won't be able to pick their arguments apart. Don't waste your time. Ignorance is truly bliss when it comes to whole life, universal life, variable universal life (VUL), and indexed universal life (IUL) insurance.

Disability Insurance

Disability insurance pays you a monthly benefit while you're disabled and you're unable to work or unable to work to the fullest extent as before. Until you're financially independent, it's very important to have both short-term and long-term disability insurance. If your employer doesn't offer disability insurance, you should buy it yourself.

I had both short-term and long-term disability insurance through my employers when I worked. When one employer didn't offer disability insurance, I bought a policy myself. I no longer have disability insurance because my family no longer depends on my income.

Employer Coverage

Short-term disability covers you for a short period of time. In some states, short-term disability coverage is mandated by state law. The short-term disability insurance offered by my last employer kicks in from day seven of disability and it pays 2/3 of an employee's monthly base pay for up to one year. If the employee recovers from his or her disability within one year, that's the end of it.

Long-term disability covers you if your disability goes beyond the short-term. The long-term disability insurance offered by my last employer picks up when short-term disability insurance ends and goes to age 65 if the employee is still disabled by then. It pays 60% of an employee's monthly base pay when his or her disability started.

2/3 or 60% of the monthly base pay isn't 100%. There's no adjustment for inflation if the disability lasts many years. Therefore, the employee has an incentive to rehabilitate and return to work, even if at a reduced capacity.

Some employers offer a choice of pre-tax or post-tax payroll deductions for disability insurance. You can have the company pay the disability insurance premium in pre-tax dollars, in which case your benefits will be taxable when you're disabled. Or you can choose to pay taxes on the premium and have the company deduct the premium in post-tax dollars, in which case your benefits won't be taxed when you're disabled.

When I had this choice, I chose post-tax. In effect, when you choose post-tax, you're buying a little more insurance. Usually, you're in a better financial position to pay taxes on the premium than you are to pay taxes on the benefits when you're disabled.

Individual Policy

For most people working at employers that offer short-term and long-term disability insurance, the employer coverage is good enough, and it's often free. If your employer doesn't offer it, you should buy an individual policy.

The best way to buy is through an insurance agent who specializes in disability insurance. The agent's commission is built into the price of the policy. You can't get the policy for any less if you don't use an agent. Before you talk to an insurance agent, you can educate yourself with several key concepts in disability insurance.

Elimination Period. The elimination period refers to the time from the onset of the disability until the insurance company starts to pay you. It's similar in concept to a deductible. If you pay for the first six months of your disability from your emergency fund, you'll pay a lower premium than if you want your disability insurance to kick in after three months.

Because you want to cover the risk of a long-lasting disability more than a short-term one, you're better off choosing a longer elimination period. Use your emergency fund to cover the elimination period.

Integration with Social Security Disability. Some disability insurance policies require integration with Social Security Disability benefits. In this type of policy, you're required to apply for Social Security Disability benefits. If you're approved for Social Security Disability, the payment from the insurance company will be reduced by your Social Security Disability benefits. You'll pay a lower premium on this type of policy.

If a policy doesn't require integration with Social Security Disability, any benefits you receive from Social Security Disability will be on top of the payments from the insurance company.

In concept I think it's fair to trade integration with Social Security Disability for a lower premium. You're trying to cover your income needs when you're disabled. You're not using your disability as an opportunity to double-dip between Social Security and private insurance.

Inflation Adjustment. If your disability lasts a long time, it's important to make sure your benefits will keep up with inflation. If you choose inflation adjustment, you'll pay a higher premium. I think it's worth it.

Own Occupation. What does it mean to be disabled? An own-occupation insurance policy will qualify you as disabled if you're unable to perform the duties of your own occupation. Some other policies will only qualify you as disabled if you aren't able to perform any occupation based on your education. Policies with a stricter own-occupation definition typically require a higher premium.

When I bought my individual disability insurance policy, I didn't chase a strict own-occupation definition. My occupation wasn't very specific. I was trying to cover my risk of not being able to work, period. I wasn't trying to collect disability insurance and then double-dip by working in another occupation. If you'd like to have disability insurance cover a very specific occupation, please discuss with your disability insurance agent.

Auto & Home Insurance

When you drive a car, you need insurance to cover your liability in case you cause an accident. When you own a home, you need insurance to cover damages to your home and your liability for accidents on your property.

Auto Insurance

Auto liability insurance is mandatory in most states. It covers your liability to others when you cause an accident. Auto insurance works differently in the following "no fault" states. I'm only describing the "traditional" system here.

Florida	Hawaii	Kansas
Kentucky	Massachusetts	Michigan
Minnesota	New Jersey	New York
North Dakota	Pennsylvania	Utah

You can also buy insurance to cover repairing your own car after an accident. For your own protection you should carry higher liability limits than the state minimum.

I have the following coverage on my auto policy through GEICO:

- Bodily Injury: $300,000 per person; $500,000 per occurrence
- Property Damage: $100,000

- Uninsured motorist bodily injury: $300,000 per person, $300,000 per occurrence
- Uninsured motorist property damage: waive the deductible for collision
- Collision: $500 deductible on a newer car; no coverage on an older car
- Comprehensive: $250 deductible on a newer car; no coverage on an older car
- Emergency road assistance: yes

The liability limits are the minimum required by my umbrella policy (see page 47). Bodily Injury coverage pays when you cause an injury to someone. The coverage limit is usually written as two numbers, for example $300,000/$500,000. The first number is per person and the second number is per occurrence. If you cause injury to two people at the same time, and your coverage limits are $300,000/$500,000, the insurance will cover claims of up to $300,000 per person and up to $500,000 for the two people combined.

Property Damage coverage pays when you damage someone's physical property, such as their cars.

Uninsured and underinsured motorist coverages pay you when an uninsured or underinsured driver causes damage to you and/or your car. Because state-mandated minimum coverages can be quite low, and some drivers don't have insurance, you should choose uninsured and underinsured motorist coverages. They're not that expensive. My premiums for uninsured and underinsured motorist coverages are about $140 a year.

Collision coverage pays for damage to your own vehicle when you're at fault. If the other party is at fault, you can claim it on your policy and then the insurance company will chase the other driver's insurance. I chose a $500 deductible because the premiums for higher deductibles aren't much less.

Comprehensive coverage protects your vehicle from theft, vandalism, hail, or other damages not caused by a collision. I chose a $250 deductible as a reasonable tradeoff between the premium and the deductible. Some insurance companies offer full glass coverage, which waives the deductible when you need to replace a damaged windshield or window.

Emergency Roadside Assistance provides towing and lockout services. The cost for this coverage through my auto insurance is much less than AAA membership fees.

Homeowner's Insurance

If you own a home, you need homeowner's insurance. It protects you from financial loss due to damages to your home by fire, hail, fallen trees, and other hazards. It also protects you from liability claims such as slips and falls, dog bites, swimming pool accidents, and so on.

The homeowner's insurance policy I have through Amica Mutual Insurance is an "HO-3" policy, which is the most common form for a single-family home. I have the following coverage on my policy:

- Dwelling: a limit determined by the size and construction of my home
- Additional amount for replacing or repairing dwelling: 30% of the dwelling limit
- Other Structure: 10% of the dwelling limit
- Personal Property: 50% of the dwelling limit
- Personal Property replacement cost: yes
- Loss of Use: 30% of the dwelling limit
- Personal Liability: $300,000 each occurrence
- Medical Payments: $1,000 each person

- Building code upgrade: 10% of the dwelling limit
- Deductible: $10,000

Dwelling coverage pays for repairing or replacing your home. The dwelling coverage limit also drives the policy limits on other coverages. The additional 30% dwelling coverage covers possible cost over-runs in repairing or replacing the home. A better policy would have no cap and pay whatever it takes to make your whole, but that's harder to find. An extra 30% is a compromise in case your dwelling coverage limit is underestimated.

The personal property coverage covers items you keep in your home, such as your furniture. The replacement cost provision pays you to replace the items, rather than the cash value for used items. It's good to have replacement cost coverage.

Personal liability coverage pays for your liability when others are hurt on your property, such as slips and falls or dog bites. $300,000 is the minimum required by my umbrella policy (see page 47).

You hope you'll never need to file a claim on your homeowner's insurance. Save it only for disasters. If you file frequent small claims, the insurance company can refuse to renew your policy. You may also have a hard time getting another insurer to take you at that time. Unfair? Maybe, but that's the reality of the homeowner's insurance landscape.

Therefore, you want a high limit, and a high deductible. I have a $10,000 deductible on my homeowner's insurance. When a disaster happens, you want to be fully protected. A high deductible lowers your premium. Since you're not going to file small claims anyway, you might as well get a high deductible and save some money on the premium.

Renter's Insurance

If you're a renter, consider buying renter's insurance. Renter's insurance is similar to homeowner's insurance except it doesn't cover the structure of the rental. It still covers items in your home and your personal liability. Some landlords require renter's insurance. In case your negligence causes damages to the rental unit, say you forgot to turn off the stove and it started a kitchen fire, the landlord can make a claim against your renter's insurance. If you don't have renter's insurance, the landlord can come after you for the damages.

Umbrella Insurance

Umbrella insurance provides additional liability coverage on top of your auto and homeowner's insurance. It pays after you exceed the liability limit on your auto or homeowner's insurance.

Say you have a serious accident that injured a pedestrian. With only your auto insurance, your liability coverage is $300,000. If you have a $1 million umbrella policy, you're covered for up to $1.3 million. Your insurance company will provide defense lawyers if the case makes it to court.

Because the umbrella policy pays only after your auto insurance or homeowner's insurance pays, you're required to raise your liability coverage on your auto and homeowner's insurance to a certain level, such as $300,000 for bodily injury on your auto policy and $300,000 for personal liability on your homeowner's policy.

The coverage limit of an umbrella policy is usually in $1 million increments. You can have a $1 million umbrella policy, a $2 million policy, $3 million, $5 million, and so on. Because the chance of having a big claim is small, the incremental cost for an additional million is smaller and smaller.

Umbrella insurance isn't that expensive. With a home and two cars, my umbrella policy from GEICO costs less than $300 per year. In today's litigious society, it's good to have good liability coverage.

Which Insurer?

Auto insurance and homeowner's insurance are regulated at the state level. The market is quite different from one state to another. Even when the same company operates in multiple states, the company can be price-competitive in one state but not in another state.

Which insurer will give you the lowest premium depends on many different factors. A company that gives your neighbor or co-worker the best rate won't necessarily give you the best rate. The only way to find out is to shop and get multiple quotes. In each state, there are sometimes 20-30 companies selling auto and homeowner's insurance. It's unrealistic for you to get a quote from each one. Somehow you need to narrow down the list of companies from which you'll request quotes.

Some states publish a "premium survey." It uses some standard profiles and shops all insurance companies doing business in the state. For example, a survey may show the rates from each company for a single male, age 31, licensed 13 years, driving a Honda Accord for 15,000 miles annually, with one speeding ticket and no at-fault accidents. I collected links to these premium surveys on my blog (see Appendix). They aren't perfect because you don't necessarily fit into one of the standard profiles. Still, they are better than nothing. Use them as one tool to help you narrow down the list of companies you contact.

Although you can have an umbrella policy from a company independent of your auto or homeowner's insurance, it's easier to get an umbrella policy from the company that also insures your car or home. Some companies won't sell you an umbrella policy unless they also insure your car or home.

Low Premium vs Honoring Claims

Most people shop for auto and homeowner's insurance based on the premium. It's easy to tell which company charges a lower premium, but it's much harder to tell how the companies handle claims. It's even more so on homeowner's insurance because claims are so rare.

If you will never have a claim, it doesn't matter which insurance company you use. Just go with the lowest premium. The point of having insurance, however, is to have the expenses covered when you do have a claim. If your insurance company fights you tooth and nail in paying a claim, you're not really saving money.

Consumer Reports consistently rates Amica and USAA as the best insurance company for claim handling (getting auto and homeowner's insurance from USAA requires military affiliation). Recently, I had an auto accident with a driver insured by Chubb. It was such a great experience in claim handling that next time my auto insurance is up for renewal, I'll get a quote from both Amica and Chubb.

Chapter 4 Health Insurance

Health insurance is a lot different than other insurance. It has some aspects of insurance, but for the most part, it's more like a tax and an entitlement. It just can't work very well if it's structured as true insurance as in life insurance, auto insurance, or homeowner's insurance.

When I worked, I had health insurance through my employer. As I'm self-employed now, I get health insurance from the Affordable Care Act (ACA) exchange from my state. When I'm 65, I'll enroll in the government's Medicare program.

Employer Health Insurance

My former employer offered several different health plans: an HMO plan, a PPO plan, and a high deductible plan. The HMO plan required using providers exclusively within the network and going through a primary care physician before seeing a specialist. The PPO plan had coverage for both in-network providers and out-of-network providers, and I could go to a specialist directly. I started with a PPO plan before I realized I was better off with the high deductible plan.

When you buy other types of insurance, such as life insurance, auto insurance, or homeowner's insurance, your premium depends on how risky the insurance company thinks you are. Factors such as being overweight and older increase the premium for your life insurance. Traffic violations or accidents increase the premium for your auto insurance, and the location of your home can increase the premium for your homeowner's insurance. If the insurance company thinks your risk is high enough, they'll even refuse to insure you.

When you have health insurance through your employer, you pay the same price whether you're healthy or not. The prices you pay vary by how many people you're covering (self only, self plus spouse, or family) and which plan you choose, but not by whether you're overweight or have high blood pressure. The employer and the insurance company treat all employees and their dependents as a group and charge a total price to cover them all. They then divide the total among the employees, regardless of health status. This makes it more like a tax and an entitlement than insurance. Everyone pays with money they would otherwise receive as their compensation and everyone gets a health plan.

The employer does it this way because if the price is determined by each employee's age and health status, those in poor health will never be able to afford it. It's too easy to figure out who will more likely incur higher healthcare expenses. According to a study by the U.S. government, 1% of the total population consumes 22% of all healthcare spending nationally. 5% of the total population consumes 50% of all spending, and the bottom 50% of the total population only consumes 3% of all healthcare spending. If you have diabetes this year, you'll still have it next year, and the following year. Some with chronic health problems were born with the problems. If health insurance is priced by the individual risk, people with chronic conditions won't be able to afford it.

Because the employer covers everyone, they spread the cost to all employees. If you're healthy, as over 90% of employees are, the price you pay for health insurance doesn't just cover your own risk. A large part of it goes to cover the small percentage of employees who aren't as healthy, similar to the taxes you pay for the good of society.

High Deductible Plan

When you realize that health insurance is more like a tax than insurance, you know it's to your financial advantage to *minimize* the amount you pay for health insurance when you're healthy. Unless you are part of the top 1% or top 5% who consume high healthcare spending, wanting "better" health insurance only means you'll pay a higher "tax" for it. If the employer offers several health plans, consider a high deductible plan that also makes you eligible for a Health Savings Account (HSA, see page 56).

When you pay the deductible in a high deductible plan, at least you're paying for your healthcare expenses. When you pay the higher premium on a more expensive health plan, a large part of the higher premium isn't for your benefits. The premiums you save every year from having a high deductible plan will help pay for the larger healthcare expenses you may have to pay out of pocket once in a while.

Here's an example of the premium cost to the employees in different insurance plans offered by one employer for family coverage.

	Traditional Plan	*High Deductible Plan*
Annual Premium	$6,682	$4,368
Employer Contribution to HSA	$0	$1,000
Deductible	$900	$3,000
Plan Pays After Deductible	90%	90%
Out of Pocket Maximum	$4,900	$7,000

In this example, if the employee's family expects to incur $5,000 in healthcare expenses, it will cost them this much out of pocket under the traditional plan:

$900 deductible + ($5,000 - $900) * 10% = $1,310

Under the high deductible plan, they'll pay this much:

$3,000 deductible - $1,000 from the employer + ($5,000 - $3,000) * 10% = $2,200

The high deductible plan will cost them $890 more ($2,200 - $1,310) in out-of-pocket expenses. However, that's still lower than the $2,300 difference in their share of the annual premium. If they incur only $2,000 in healthcare expenses instead of $5,000, they'll save even more.

The high deductible plan can cost less even if the family has unexpectedly high healthcare expenses. If this family incurs $50,000 in healthcare expenses, it will cost them this much out of pocket under the traditional plan:

$900 deductible + ($50,000 - $900) * 10% = $5,810

Because $5,810 exceeds the $4,900 out-of-pocket maximum, this family will pay $4,900 out of pocket under the traditional plan. Under the high deductible plan, they'll pay this much:

$3,000 deductible + ($50,000 - $3,000) * 10% = $7,700

Because $7,700 exceeds the $7,000 out-of-pocket maximum, this family will pay $7,000 out of pocket under the high deductible plan. Because the employer contributes $1,000 to the HSA, their net out-of-pocket expenses will be $6,000. That's $1,100 higher than the $4,900 number under the traditional plan, which is still lower than the $2,300 difference in their share of the annual premium. It doesn't make sense to pay $2,300 more in insurance premium only to save $1,100 when the healthcare expenses are unusually high.

I have a calculator on my blog that can help you calculate which health plan is better for you based on the prices for each plan and your expected healthcare expenses. See Appendix for a link to the calculator.

Cost Estimator

When you have a high deductible plan, because you'll pay 100% out of pocket except for preventive care before you meet the deductible, you're motivated to get services from cost-effective providers. Prices for the same healthcare service from different providers can easily vary by 500%. When you're about to spend $500, $1,000, or $3,000 on something, you should shop around, just as you would with any purchase.

Many don't know their insurance companies already provide a cost estimator tool to show the prices at different providers in the network, similar to how Kayak displays prices from different airlines. The tool is based on your specific insurance plan. It helps you narrow down the more cost-effective providers. Major insurance companies such as UnitedHealthcare, Blue Cross/Blue Shield, Cigna, Aetna, Humana, and Kaiser Permanente all have an online tool like this. Google the name of your insurance company and "cost estimator" to find it.

By using the cost estimator tool from my insurance company, I was able to save $500 on an MRI over having it done at the in-house facility that my doctor normally orders from.

GoodRx

When you have a high deductible plan, you also pay 100% out of pocket on prescription drugs before you meet the deductible. Prescription drug prices can also vary by several times at different pharmacies. Sometimes prices are higher with insurance than without. When it's the same medication, why pay more?

GoodRx (goodrx.com) shows you prescription drug prices at different pharmacies near you. It's great to know a baseline price. If the price you get going through insurance is much higher, you can use the discount codes in GoodRx and pay the lower price. Buying through GoodRx won't count toward your insurance deductible. Still, when you have substantial savings and don't expect to meet the deductible anyway, it's well worth not counting toward the deductible.

Health Savings Account (HSA)

Because I choose an eligible high deductible health plan, I'm allowed to contribute to a Health Savings Account (HSA). I contribute the maximum possible to the HSA every year.

Triple Tax-Free

You put pre-tax money into the HSA. Unlike the health FSA (see page 62), the HSA doesn't have a "use it or lose it" rule; the money in the HSA is always yours. You can invest the money for additional growth. While the money stays in the HSA, it grows tax-free. When you take it out to pay for qualified healthcare expenses, it's again tax-free. Because the money goes in pre-tax, grows tax-free inside the account, and it comes out tax-free, the HSA is said to be "triple tax-free."

The catch is that you must have an eligible high deductible health plan in order to contribute to an HSA and you must have no other medical coverage (dental and vision plans don't count as medical coverage). If you're married, you can't be simultaneously covered under your spouse's plan unless that plan is also an HSA-eligible high deductible plan. You and your spouse also can't have a general-purpose health FSA (see page 62), because a general-purpose health FSA also counts as other coverage.

Not all high deductible health plans are HSA-eligible. The plan must also meet other IRS requirements. Just having a high deductible isn't enough. If you'd like to contribute to an HSA, make sure your health plan is HSA-eligible, and make sure you don't have other coverage, including a general-purpose health FSA from your spouse.

An HSA-eligible plan is usually clearly labeled as such. If you see a plan with a high deductible but it doesn't say anything about the HSA, it's likely not HSA-eligible. The best way to double-check is to call the health insurance plan's customer service and ask.

Contribution Limit

Because you get triple tax-free benefits with an HSA, besides requiring an HSA-eligible health plan with no other coverage, Congress also set a limit on how much you can contribute to an HSA each year. The contribution limit depends on whether your HSA-eligible health plan covers just one person ("single") or more than one person ("family"). The contribution limit adjusts with inflation each year. In 2020, it's $3,550 for single coverage and $7,100 for family coverage. If you are 55 or older by the end of the year, you can put in an additional $1,000 as a "catch-up" contribution. You don't have to be working to contribute to an HSA. Retirees can also contribute to an HSA as long as their only health insurance is an eligible high deductible plan.

An HSA is only in one person's name. There are no joint HSAs. If a married couple has separate individual HSA-eligible health plans, they must contribute to separate HSAs, each in their individual name.

If a married couple has a family health plan under one person's name, they can either contribute at the family coverage level to only one person's HSA, or divide up the family coverage contribution limit however they want and contribute to two separate HSAs.

If one spouse has single coverage and the other spouse has family coverage, they are treated as both having family coverage and they can divide up the family coverage contribution limit between them however they want, but together they still have only one combined family coverage limit ($7,100 in 2020).

If your family high deductible plan covers an adult child who isn't a dependent on your tax return, both you and the adult child can contribute at the family coverage level to separate HSAs.

For those 55 or older, if they'd like to contribute their additional $1,000 catch-up, they'll have to contribute the catch-up to the HSA in their name. Only the person who's 55 or older by the end of the year can contribute the catch-up. If they have a family plan and they normally contribute to the HSA in the name of one spouse, the other spouse will have to open a separate HSA for the $1,000 catch-up.

> **Example**: Brad and Jane are covered under an HSA-eligible health plan through Jane's employer. They are contributing to Jane's HSA at the family coverage level. Both Brad and Jane are 55 by the end of the year. Jane can contribute $8,100 to her HSA in 2020 ($7,100 family coverage limit plus her $1,000 catch-up). Brad can contribute another $1,000 catch-up to an HSA in his name.

It gets a little tricky when your health insurance changes mid-year. Basically, the contribution limit is prorated each month. If you have an HSA-eligible high deductible plan on the first of any month, you get 1/12th of the annual contribution limit for that month. If your plan covers only one person, it's 1/12th of the single coverage limit. If your plan covers more than one person, it's 1/12th of the family coverage limit. Because Medicare isn't a high deductible plan, once you start Medicare you can no longer contribute to an HSA, but your spouse still can if he or she isn't on Medicare.

For example, if you start out with family coverage for 3 months and then you drop down to single coverage for 9 months, your contribution limit for the year is 3/12th of the family coverage limit plus 9/12th of the single coverage limit. If you didn't have an HSA-eligible plan in the first part of the year and you start a new job that offers one, your contribution limit for the year is prorated by the number of months you have the eligible high deductible plan.

There is a "last month rule" that can override the prorated calculation. Invoking the "last month rule" makes you eligible to contribute to the full year limit when you have an HSA-eligible plan on the first of December, but the rule comes with its own complexities. I don't think it's worth invoking the "last month rule" just to squeeze out a few more months of contributions. I suggest you stay with the prorated calculation and forget that the "last month rule" exists.

If you see that you contributed too much to your HSA based on these contribution limits, the HSA provider has a special procedure to withdraw the excess contribution. You must follow the specific procedure and not withdraw on your own, otherwise it only counts as a normal withdrawal, not withdrawing the excess contribution.

Through Employer and On Your Own

When I had an HSA-eligible high deductible plan through my employer, my employer also put some money into my HSA. Many employers do this. If you're married and both your employers offer an HSA-eligible plan, it can be to your advantage to enroll in separate plans to get the HSA money from both employers. Since the employer contribution counts toward your annual contribution limit, you'll have to reduce your contribution accordingly.

When you contribute to an HSA through your employer, most companies have it set up such that your contributions are deducted before federal income tax, before state income tax in most states (except California and New Jersey), and before Social Security and Medicare taxes. If you contribute to an HSA outside your employer, you can claim a deduction on your tax return but you'll have to pay

Social Security and Medicare taxes. It's better to contribute through your employer if you can.

Many HSA providers let you invest the money in your HSA. If you don't like the investment options at your employer's HSA provider, you can transfer or roll over the money from your employer's HSA provider to a provider of your choice. You can keep the HSA through your employer open for new contributions but transfer or roll over the existing balance to another HSA, say once a year, for access to better investment options.

A transfer happens between two HSA providers directly. There is no limit on the frequency of HSA transfers from one provider to another. You fill out a transfer form from the receiving provider and they'll request the transfer from the sending provider. Some HSA providers charge a fee (for example $30) for doing the outbound transfer.

A rollover happens when you take the money out of one HSA, put it into your own bank account, and then make a deposit to another HSA. Usually there is no fee if you do a rollover, but you can only do one rollover every rolling one-year period. If you started a rollover this year on June 5th, you can only start a new rollover after June 6th next year. Although you don't pay any tax on the rollover, the rollover must be reported on your tax return.

To do a rollover, you request a check or electronic funds transfer from the current HSA provider. You put the money into your own bank account. Then you make a deposit within 60 days to the new HSA provider. You attach a rollover contribution form to indicate it's a rollover.

The best place to have an HSA is Fidelity Investments (fidelity.com). Fidelity doesn't charge any maintenance fee on HSA accounts. You can invest in practically anything that's available in a Fidelity account. See Chapter 8 for more information on investing.

When I worked, I contributed to the HSA through my employer. After I reimbursed myself for all eligible expenses for the year, I rolled over the remaining balance to another HSA to have the leftover money invested. I then repeated this pattern the following year. I did this because the employer's HSA provider charged high fees for investing the leftover balance.

Reimbursing Expenses

Putting money into the HSA and taking money out of the HSA are totally separate. Regardless of whose name the HSA is in, the money in the HSA can be used to reimburse qualified medical expenses incurred by the HSA owner, spouse, or dependents. When you no longer have an HSA-eligible high deductible plan, the money in the HSA can still be used to reimburse qualified medical expenses. You only can't contribute new money to the HSA until you have an HSA-eligible high deductible plan again.

When you reimburse yourself for qualified medical expenses, you request a transfer from the HSA to your personal bank account. Some HSA providers issue an HSA debit card. I don't use it because (a) it's another card to carry in the wallet; (b) it doesn't earn rewards; and (c) healthcare expenses often aren't final at the time of service. If you paid with an HSA debit card and it turns out to be too much after insurance adjustments, it can be a hassle to put the money back into the HSA and not have it count as a new contribution.

You don't have to submit receipts to the HSA provider. You only keep the receipts for your tax records. There is no deadline for requesting reimbursements. While it's possible to save the receipts, not reimburse from the HSA, and let the entire balance in the HSA grow, I choose to reimburse each year. This is "good enough" for me. Keeping track of old expenses for many years will require too much attention.

Flexible Spending Account (FSA)

My former employer also offered a health Flexible Spending Account (FSA). Before I switched to a high deductible plan, I used a health FSA to cover my out-of-pocket healthcare expenses, because only a high deductible plan qualifies for an HSA. After I also contributed to an HSA, I used a limited-purpose FSA to cover only dental and vision expenses.

You have to decide up-front during open enrollment for the following year how much you'll contribute to the FSA. With few exceptions, this decision can't be changed after open enrollment ends. The benefit of putting money into the FSA is that the money will be deducted from your pay before federal and state income taxes and also before Social Security and Medicare taxes. After you incur eligible healthcare expenses, you can claim reimbursement from the FSA. The reimbursement is tax-free.

Because you're spending pre-tax money, the IRS sets a limit on how much you can contribute to the FSA. That limit is adjusted with inflation every year. In 2020, the contribution limit is $2,750 per employee. If you're married and both of your employers offer an FSA, each of you can contribute up to the annual maximum independently.

The money in the FSA can be used to pay for eligible healthcare expenses by you, your spouse, and your dependents, whether or not they are on the same health plan as you. A *general-purpose FSA* can reimburse out-of-pocket expenses not covered by medical insurance (your deductible and co-pays) and dental and vision expenses. A *limited-purpose FSA*, designed to be used in conjunction with an HSA, can reimburse only dental and vision expenses. When I also contributed to an HSA, I had a limited-purpose FSA for dental and vision expenses only.

Some FSA providers give you a debit card, with which you can pay for eligible expenses directly. You're still supposed to keep all the receipts when you use the FSA debit card. The FSA provider can come back and ask you for receipts to substantiate the expenses. I find it much easier to pay for the expenses myself and request reimbursement with the receipts. By using my credit card, I also earn some rewards.

The downside of the FSA is the "use it or lose it" rule. If you over-estimated your out-of-pocket expenses, any money not spent at the end of the year can be forfeited. Some plans allow carrying over up to $500 to the next year. Some plans allow a grace period until March 15 the next year to spend down the money. Some plans don't offer any carryover or grace period.

If you leave your employer mid-year, the money in the FSA can only reimburse expenses incurred on or before your termination date. Any additional money will be forfeited. On the other hand, the annual amount you elected at open enrollment is available for reimbursement on day one. If you requested more reimbursement than your payroll deductions by the time you leave, you won't have to pay back the difference.

If your health insurance doesn't make you eligible to contribute to an HSA, you get tax benefits from contributing to an FSA to cover your out-of-pocket expenses. If you already contribute to an HSA, using a limited-purpose FSA on top of an HSA for only dental and vision expenses leaves more money in the HSA for future growth. Even if you over-estimated and you end up forfeiting some money, you can still be better off by putting money in the FSA than not choosing it at all. You'll be fine if you estimate conservatively.

Dependent Care Flexible Spending Account

Dependent Care Flexible Spending Account (dependent care FSA) isn't really related to health insurance but because it's a close cousin of the health FSA, I'm mentioning it here.

You can use a dependent care FSA only if your employer offers it. Money put into the dependent care FSA can be used to pay for eligible childcare expenses, such as daycare, baby sitter, nanny, and pre-school. These expenses must be incurred so that you can work. If you're married, both you and your spouse must be working, be a full-time student, actively looking for work, or incapable of providing care to your child.

Similar to the health FSA, you choose how much you will contribute to the dependent care FSA during open enrollment for the following year. The money goes in before federal and state income taxes and also before Social Security and Medicare taxes. The IRS sets the contribution limit for each year. The limit for 2020 is $5,000. If you're married, the two of you can contribute up to $5,000 a year *combined*, not $5,000 each person.

If you have eligible childcare expenses, it would be a no-brainer to use a dependent care FSA. Because childcare expenses are more predictable than healthcare expenses, there would be less of an issue with the "use it or lose it" rule. Unlike health FSA, when you leave your employer mid-year, you can still request reimbursement for expenses incurred through the end of the year.

Health Reimbursement Account (HRA)

Some employers offer a Health Reimbursement Account (HRA). Similar to a health FSA, you can use the money in the HRA to pay for your out-of-pocket healthcare expenses. Reimbursements from the HRA are tax-free. Unlike a health FSA, only the employer contributes to the HRA; you don't. There is also not a "use it or lose it" rule. The money in the HRA automatically rolls over to the next year. When you leave the employer, any unused HRA money is forfeited.

Employers set the rules on their HRAs. Some HRAs can cover healthcare expenses incurred by you, spouse, and dependents, whether or not they are on the employer's health plan. Some HRAs only cover healthcare expenses by those who are on the employer's health plan.

Having a general-purpose HRA counts having other healthcare coverage, which makes you ineligible to contribute to an HSA. When you also contribute to an HSA, you can have a limited-purpose HRA, which covers only dental and vision expenses.

COBRA

COBRA is the name of a federal law that requires employers to offer health insurance to former employees for up to 18 months after they leave. That sounds great until you see the prices. In an employer health plan, employees typically pay 25-30% of the total premium. In COBRA, former employees pay 100% of the total premium plus up to 2% administrative fee. As a result, the prices for COBRA are three to four times the prices for active employees. In addition, the COBRA premiums are paid with post-tax dollars, whereas the payroll deductions for active employees are pre-tax.

COBRA can be useful when you're in between jobs for a short period. If you don't qualify for a premium tax credit for an ACA plan (see the next section), COBRA can still be less expensive than an ACA plan. After I left my employer, I used COBRA for dental and vision coverage for 18 months because the COBRA prices were still lower than the prices for plans I could buy elsewhere.

One good feature of COBRA is that you have 60 days to elect COBRA and the election will be retroactive. Suppose your health insurance through your former employer ends on April 30. You have 60 days from that date to sign up for COBRA. If you have new health insurance before 60 days are up, and you don't incur large healthcare expenses during the gap, you can skip COBRA and not pay the high COBRA premium. If you incur large healthcare expenses during the gap, you can sign up for COBRA before the 60-day deadline, pay the premium, and have COBRA coverage retroactive from May 1.

Affordable Care Act (ACA)

When you're self-employed, unemployed, or when your employer doesn't offer health insurance, you can buy health insurance from an exchange set up by the government under the Affordable Care Act (ACA), also known as Obamacare. As I'm self-employed now, I've been on an ACA plan in the last three years.

The principles of ACA plans are relatively straight forward. The details can be quite complex. The short story is that ACA creates two different worlds. If your income is low enough, you'll get a tax credit to help you pay for health insurance. If your income is higher than the cutoff set by the government, you're totally on your own.

The availability of plans and prices vary greatly by region. You go online to an ACA exchange to check plans and prices for your zip code. Some states operate their own exchange. For example, the exchange for California is called Covered California (coveredca.com). Other states use the healthcare.gov exchange operated by the federal government. This web page from healthcare.gov lists the exchange for each state:

www.healthcare.gov/marketplace-in-your-state

Plans offered on the ACA exchange are categorized into Bronze, Silver, Gold, and Platinum tiers. Among plans offered by the same insurer, Bronze plans cover less and cost less than Silver plans, which cover less and cost less than Gold plans, and so on. Within each tier, the deductible, co-pay, and out-of-pocket maximum are similar but the prices among different insurers can be a lot different. For example, here are the different coverage tiers in my area for a family plan:

	Deductible	Hospital Co-Pay	Out of Pocket Maximum
Bronze	$12,600	40%	$15,600
Silver	$8,000	20%	$15,600
Gold	$0	20%	$15,600
Platinum	$0	$250/day	$9,000

I chose a high deductible Bronze plan to keep the cost low.

Premium Tax Credit

The government only provides a tax credit when your income is below a cutoff. The income being measured is your Modified Adjusted Gross Income (MAGI), which is basically the Adjusted Gross Income on your tax return plus tax-exempt municipal bond interest and any untaxed Social Security benefits.

ACA looks at your household income and compares it with the Federal Poverty Level (FPL) for your household size. Here are the FPL numbers for 2020 coverage in the lower 48 states (the numbers are higher in Hawaii and Alaska):

Household Size	Federal Poverty Level
1	$12,490
2	$16,910
3	$21,330
4	$25,750
more	Add $4,420 each

Suppose you have two people in your household in the lower 48 states, and your MAGI is $50,000. Your income is 296% of FPL for your household size:

$$\$50,000 \ / \ \$16,910 = 2.96$$

ACA then says at each income level relative to the FPL, you're expected to pay a set percentage of your income toward the annual cost of the second lowest cost Silver plan in your area. The federal government will make up for any shortfall in the form of a premium tax credit. The applicable percentages for 2020 look like this:

Income	Applicable Percentage
< 133% FPL	2.06%
133% - 150% FPL	3.09% − 4.12%
150% - 200% FPL	4.12% − 6.49%
200% - 250% FPL	6.49% − 8.29%
250% - 300% FPL	8.29% − 9.78%
300% - 400% FPL	9.78%
> 400% FPL	no premium tax credit

In our example, your household income is 296% FPL. This translates to an applicable percentage of 9.66% through linear extrapolation in the 250% - 300% FPL range:

$$8.29\% + (296 - 250) \ / \ (300 - 250) * (9.78\% - 8.29\%) = 9.66\%$$

It means you're expected to pay 9.66% of your income toward a second lowest cost Silver plan in your area. That's $50,000 * 9.66% = $4,830 in 2020.

Suppose you have five Silver plans in your area, which charge the following annual premiums:

- Plan #1: $1,128/month ($13,536/year)
- Plan #2: $1,341/month ($16,092/year)
- Plan #3: $1,451/month ($17,412/year)
- Plan #4: $1,567/month ($18,804/year)

- Plan #5: $2,088/month ($25,056/year)

Your second lowest cost Silver plan is Plan #2, which charges $1,341/month or $16,092/year. When the second lowest cost Silver plan costs $16,092/year and you're only expected to pay $4,830 toward it, the government will give you the difference as a premium tax credit:

$$\$16,092 - \$4,830 = \$11,262$$

You're not limited to choosing the second lowest cost Silver plan in your area. It's only used to calculate the premium tax credit. The government will give you up to $11,262 in premium tax credit for ACA health insurance regardless of which plan you actually choose. If you enroll in a less expensive Bronze plan, you keep 100% of the price difference between the less expensive Bronze plan and the second lowest cost Silver plan. If you pick a more expensive Gold plan, you pay 100% of the price difference between the more expensive Gold plan and the second lowest cost Silver plan.

Suppose the Bronze plan you choose costs $12,984 a year, after the same $11,262 premium tax credit from the government, you only pay $12,984 - $11,262 = $1,722 for the year as opposed to $4,830 if you choose the second lowest cost Silver plan. Suppose the Gold plan you want costs $18,300 a year, now you'll have to pay $18,300 - $11,262 = $7,038 for the year.

Receiving a premium tax credit is also referred to as getting a subsidy for buying health insurance under the ACA. The government will make an advance payment to the insurance company based on an estimate of the next year's income you give at open enrollment. It's like getting an interest-free loan from the government. You use the loan to pay your health insurance premium. When you file your taxes next year, you pay back the loan with your premium tax credit.

Because the advance payment from the government is only based on an estimate of your income, and you can never be sure what your actual income will be until you file your taxes, the advance payment will differ from the premium tax credit based on your actual income. If your actual income comes in lower than the estimate, which results in a higher premium tax credit, you'll receive the difference when you file your tax return. If your actual income comes in higher than the estimate, which results in a lower premium tax credit, you'll pay the difference when you file your tax return, with a cap on the repayment. If you thought you would qualify for the premium tax credit but it turns out you're not eligible, you'll have to pay back the entire advance payment, which can be over $10,000.

Cost Sharing Reductions

If your estimated income is at 250% FPL or below, in addition to the premium tax credit, ACA gives another subsidy in the form of a lower deductible, lower co-pays, and a lower out-of-pocket maximum than in the standard plans. It's called Cost Sharing Reductions (CSR).

CSR is only on Silver plans. If your estimated income is at 250% FPL or below, you can choose an enhanced version of a Silver plan. The enhancements get further enhanced at lower income levels. Here are the standard and enhanced Silver plans for a single person in my area:

Standard Silver Plan	Deductible: $4,000
	Primary care office visit co-pay: $40
	Out-of-pocket maximum: $7,800
250% FPL or below	Deductible: $3,700
	Primary care office visit co-pay: $35
	Out-of-pocket maximum: $6,500
200% FPL or below	Deductible: $1,400
	Primary care office visit co-pay: $15
	Out-of-pocket maximum: $2,700

150% FPL or below	Deductible: $75
	Primary care office visit co-pay: $5
	Out-of-pocket maximum: $1,000

As you can see, the Silver plan first gets slightly enhanced at 250% FPL. As your incomes goes below 200% FPL, the benefits are much better. When your income goes below 150% FPL, the benefits get better still.

The premium tax credit and the cost sharing reductions help people with lower income afford health insurance.

Over the Cliff

It's quite a different story at higher income levels. The premium tax credit stops at 400% FPL. In our example of a household size of two people in the lower 48 states, 400% FPL is $67,640 in 2020. If your income during the year is exactly $67,640, and if the second lowest cost Silver plan in your area costs $16,000 a year, you'll receive a premium tax credit of $16,000 - $67,640 * 9.78% = $9,385. If the price for the second lowest cost Silver plan in your area goes up by $2,000, your premium tax credit will also go up by $2,000. As long as you keep your income below 400% FPL, you're effectively shielded from health insurance premium increases.

However, if your income is higher than $67,640, all of a sudden, your premium tax credit disappears. Earning $1 more will make you pay thousands more for your health insurance. You also lose the shield for health insurance price increases. If the plan costs $16,000 a year, you'll pay $16,000. If the plan costs $18,000 next year, you'll have to pay $18,000.

Therefore, when you get health insurance from the ACA exchange, do everything you can to keep your income below 400% FPL. Unless your income is low enough to qualify you for the cost sharing reductions, consider buying a Bronze plan to keep the cost low.

Medicare

Medicare is the federal government's health insurance program for seniors. I'll be eligible for Medicare when I'm 65. When that day comes, I'll sign up in a heartbeat.

Medicare isn't entirely free, and it doesn't cover everything. When you enroll and become a Medicare beneficiary, you must still pay monthly premiums to cover physician services and prescription drugs. 95% of Medicare beneficiaries pay the standard premiums, which reflect only 25% of the program costs. The federal government pays the other 75% of the costs from Medicare taxes paid by workers. After paying Medicare taxes to support the older generations, you finally get to be supported by younger generations. Paying Medicare premiums is a good deal.

Original Medicare and Medigap

Medicare is divided into Original Medicare and Medicare Advantage programs. You have to choose between Original Medicare and Medicare Advantage. With Original Medicare, you can use any provider that accepts Medicare. In a Medicare Advantage program, you limit yourself to the providers within that program (like an HMO in private insurance) in exchange for better coverage than Original Medicare.

Original Medicare consists of Part A, Part B, and Part D. Part A covers hospital services. Part B covers physician services. Part D covers prescription drugs. Part A is free. Part B and Part D require a premium payment. If you don't sign up for Part B and Part D when you're first eligible and you don't have an allowable excuse, you'll face late enrollment penalties in the form of higher premiums for life.

You have many choices in Part D prescription drug plans. Different Part D plans cover different prescription drugs differently. You choose the Part D plan for next year during the open enrollment period. The best Part D plan for you in one year may not be the best plan for you in another year.

Original Medicare doesn't have an out-of-pocket maximum. When Medicare pays 80% for an expense, your 20% share isn't capped to any dollar amount in a calendar year. If your treatment costs $1 million, you can be on the hook for 20% of that $1 million. As a result, many people on Original Medicare also buy Medicare Supplement Insurance ("Medigap" plan) to cover the portions that Original Medicare doesn't pay.

Medigap plans aren't subsidized by taxes. The standardized Medigap policies fall into several plan categories, such as Medigap Plan A, Plan B, Plan D, Plan G, etc. (not to be confused with Medicare Part A, Part B, and Part D). Some Medigap plans provide more benefits than others. People who have more severe health issues will buy more comprehensive Medigap plans, which make those plans more expensive. If you're healthy, you're still better off minimizing the premium you pay for Medigap plans.

Medicare Advantage

Insurance companies create Medicare Advantage programs that take Medicare funding from the government and provide benefits to Medicare beneficiaries. This is similar in concept to charter schools in education. Specific Medicare Advantage program benefits and costs vary. Some Medicare Advantage programs don't cost any more than Original Medicare. Some programs add extra premiums for enhanced benefits. Some programs include benefits that aren't in Original Medicare, such as coverage for hearing, dental, and vision expenses.

Navigating Medicare Decisions

With different options in different Medicare prescription drug programs, Medigap plans, Medicare Advantage programs, and rules on switching between different programs, it can get very confusing. Each state has a State Health Insurance Assistance Program (SHIP) with trained counselors who provide free assistance in understanding and navigating the programs. You can locate the SHIP services for your state at shiptacenter.org. When I get close to age 65, I'll speak to a SHIP counselor.

A private company called i65 (i65.com) seeks to provide clarity and help people make informed choices on Medicare. The i65 tool costs $65 and provides reports on different choices in your area. It's worth a shot as an additional resource.

Long Term Care

Long Term Care is related to health insurance but it's not really health insurance. Long Term Care covers expenses for assisting your activities of daily living – eating, bathing, dressing, going to the bathroom, and getting in and out of a bed. Even though these services are needed predominantly when you're older, Medicare doesn't cover long-term care. Medicaid, the government's health insurance program for low-income people, covers long-term care but you'd have to use up your assets and become low-income first. The costs of long-term care consume a significant share of Medicaid funding. According to a report in Health Affairs, 40% of Medicaid funding went to cover 6% of Medicaid enrollees who used long-term care.

You can buy Long Term Care insurance in the private market. However, the Long Term Care insurance market isn't working very well right now. The long-term care needs are higher at older ages. If you wait until you're older, the premiums are super-high and you may also have a hard time qualifying for Long Term Care insurance. If you buy at a younger age, your premiums aren't locked in. Many policyholders have faced 30%, 50%, or 100% premium increases in recent years. They are put in a no-win situation. If they don't renew, they would've overpaid for their Long Term Care insurance for many years because their chances of needing long-term care in those early years were slim. If they renew, the new premiums are unaffordable, and the premiums may increase yet again in the future.

It's a difficult situation. My wife and I decided to save and invest money on our own for long-term care. If we need long-term care, we will use the money. If we don't, our families will get it.

Chapter 5 Workplace Retirement Plans

Your employer may offer one or more types of retirement plans: 401(k), 403(b), 401(a), 457, SIMPLE IRA, SEP-IRA, pension, cash balance plan, and deferred compensation plan. Participating in these plans is the best way to save for retirement because you get tax benefits. This chapter covers the various types of workplace retirement plans. Chapter 8 covers investing in these plans and in other accounts.

401(k), 403(b), TSP

Many employers in the private sector offer 401(k) plans. Public schools and non-profit employers offer 403(b) plans. The federal government offers the Thrift Savings Plan (TSP). They are very similar. A 401(k), 403(b), or TSP offers tax-deferred or tax-free savings through convenient and consistent payroll deductions. Many employers also chip in. They can match your contributions, or they can contribute unconditionally. Because there is a tax penalty for taking the money out before age 59-1/2, it forces you to invest for the long term. It's a great way to save money for your retirement.

Contribute the Maximum Allowed

The tax-deferred or tax-free savings are such a great deal that the law limits how much money can be contributed to these plans.

The first limit, called the *elective deferral limit*, is on the employee. As an employee, you can contribute a maximum of $19,500 in 2020 to all 401(k) and 403(b) plans across all employers. If you are 50 or over by the end of the year, you can contribute an additional $6,500 in 2020. These limits are adjusted for inflation in

$500 increments. The employer contributions are not included in these limits.

The second limit, called the *annual additions limit*, is on the employer. Across all plans sponsored by an employer, a maximum of $57,000 can be added on behalf of an employee in 2020. This includes both the employee's contributions and the employer's contributions. This limit is *per employer*. If you have multiple unrelated employers, and they are generous enough, you can have up to $57,000 contributed separately to your account at each employer in 2020.

Both the elective deferral limit and the annual additions limit follow the "use it or lose it" rule. If you contribute less than the maximum allowed in one year, you don't get to carry over your headroom to future years. My first rule in using a 401(k) or 403(b) plan is simply *contribute the maximum allowed every year*. Both my wife and I followed this rule since our very first full-time job.

Don't contribute just enough to get the employer match. Contribute the maximum you're allowed. When you get used to the smaller paychecks, you won't miss the money. When you look back years later, you'll see a nice sum of money saved up in the plan.

Everything else is secondary to contributing the maximum allowed to the plan. How you should invest the money matters, but not as much as contributing more. Suppose Person A contributes $5,000 a year to get a 50% employer match and Person B contributes the $19,500 maximum. If Person A earns 6% return per year and Person B earns only 4% return per year, by the end of 30 years, Person A still only has less than 1/2 of the amount as Person B. Even if the investment options in your plan aren't so great, you should still contribute the maximum. You'll have an opportunity to move the money elsewhere for better investment options when you switch jobs (see "rollovers" on page 83).

If you're not able to contribute the maximum allowed just yet, make it a goal and work toward it. This will have the greatest impact on the amount available for your retirement.

Favor Traditional Over Roth

Many workplace retirement plans give you a choice between making Traditional and Roth contributions. When you choose Traditional, the contributions come out of your paychecks pre-tax. The money you earn in the plan also stays pre-tax. When you take the money out after you retire, you pay taxes at that time. When you choose Roth contributions, the contributions come out of your paychecks post-tax. The money you earn in the Roth account is tax-free. When you take the money out after age 59-1/2, it's tax-free. Employer contributions always go into the Traditional account.

	Traditional	*Roth*
Contributions	pre-tax	post-tax
Earnings	tax-deferred	tax-free
Withdrawals	taxable	tax-free

The annual maximum contribution limit is shared between Traditional and Roth contributions. If you choose to contribute the annual maximum as Traditional, you'll use up the limit and not be able to make any Roth contributions. If you choose to contribute some as Roth, you'll have to reduce your Traditional contributions.

When your 401(k) or 403(b) plan offers both a Traditional pre-tax option and a Roth option, consider choosing 100% Traditional by default, unless you have a strong reason for contributing some as Roth. I always chose 100% Traditional in my 401(k) plans.

You should choose Traditional by default because when you're working, you tend to be in a higher tax bracket than when you're not working. The pre-tax money is deducted off the top from your highest tax bracket. When you retire, the money you receive from the plan first goes into the lower tax brackets before it reaches the top.

Picture water in a bucket, representing your income, with lines on the side of the bucket marking different tax brackets. When you make Traditional pre-tax contributions to the 401(k) or 403(b) plan, you scoop water from the top of the bucket. That's how money is deducted from your paychecks: from the highest tax bracket.

When you retire, you have an empty bucket. You pour water into it. The water first covers the bottom of the bucket. That part of the money isn't taxed because of deductions. As water fills up the bucket, it goes through the lower tax brackets first before reaching the top.

In addition, states with higher paying jobs tend to have higher state income taxes. When you make Traditional pre-tax contributions, the contributions are exempt from state income tax as well (except in a handful of states). When you retire, you don't necessarily retire in states where you worked. If you retire in a state with no or low state income tax, you'll have escaped those higher state income taxes.

Of course there are always exceptions to this rule, such as doctors in resident training making a low income now and anticipating much higher income later, or public service employees with a great pension that will cover the lower tax brackets in retirement. They should consider making Roth contributions. Unless you clearly fall into an exception, favor Traditional over Roth.

Spread Your Contributions Through the Full Year

When you receive an employer match to your 401(k), 403(b), or TSP contributions, many employers calculate the match on a "per pay period" basis. In each pay period, if you contribute at least a certain percentage of your pay, the employer will match your contributions. If you don't contribute in that pay period, the employer won't match.

If your employer operates this way, it creates a problem when your contributions stop in the middle of the year because you reached your annual maximum. When your contributions stop, the employer match also stops. You'll have received less than the full match for the year.

Some employers mitigate this problem by doing a "true-up" match in the following year. If you received less than the full match because your contributions stopped too soon, the employer will give you an additional match to make you whole. However, some employers require that you must stay through the end of the year in order to receive the "true-up" match; if you left you don't get it.

Because not all employers give a "true-up" match and because there's a risk you won't get it when you leave, it's better to spread your contributions throughout the year and make sure you contribute at least the minimum percentage of pay for the full match in every pay period. If your employer matches on 6% of your pay, make sure you contribute at least 6% of your pay in every pay period and don't max out for the year too soon.

Non-Roth After-Tax Contributions

In addition to Traditional pre-tax and Roth contributions, some 401(k) or 403(b) plans also allow non-Roth after-tax contributions. These after-tax contributions are not the same as Roth contributions even though they both use after-tax money. The difference here is that non-Roth after-tax contributions are above and beyond the elective deferral limit for Traditional and Roth contributions, whereas Traditional and Roth contributions share one single contribution limit.

For example, when the annual contribution limit for Traditional and Roth contributions is $19,500 in 2020 and you decide to contribute $19,500 as Traditional, you can't contribute any more as Roth, but if the plan offers the option, you can still make non-Roth after-tax contributions. For someone under 50, the maximum contribution limit for all types of contributions at one single employer, including employer contributions, is $57,000 in 2020. When the employer contributes $4,000, you can put in this much as non-Roth after-tax contributions:

$$\$57,000 - \$19,500 - \$4,000 = \$33,500$$

If your plan offers the non-Roth after-tax contribution option, it's possible that the contributions can be rolled over to the Roth portion within the plan (via an *In-plan Roth Rollover*). Or they can be withdrawn to a Roth IRA (see the next chapter) via an *In-Service Distribution*. If your plan offers either option for the non-Roth after-tax contributions, once the money enters a Roth account, the future earnings will be tax-free. This move is known unofficially as a *"mega backdoor Roth."*

When you do the In-plan Roth Rollover or the In-Service Distribution, you don't pay tax again on the non-Roth after-tax contributions. You pay tax only on the earnings associated with the contributions. The earnings will be small if you do the rollover or distribution shortly after you make the contributions.

This great feature of the 401(k) or 403(b) plan enables a high contribution to a Roth account in the plan on top of the normal 401(k) contributions. If your plan offers it, *contribute the maximum allowed*.

More and more companies are offering non-Roth after-tax contributions together with In-plan Roth Rollovers or In-Service Distributions. Some plans are set up to do automatic In-plan Roth Rollovers. As soon as the plan sees non-Roth after-tax contributions, the money is rolled over to the Roth account within the plan the next day. My former employer's plan added the non-Roth after-tax option. Had I not left, I would've contributed the maximum allowed.

Rollovers

When you switch jobs, you have the option to leave the money in your previous employer's plan. As long as your balance is over $5,000, the plan can't kick you out. However, you may want to move the money to a new place, lest you forget you still have money in the old plan.

You can move the money to your new employer's plan or you can move it to an IRA (see the next chapter). Either way will keep the retirement plan money in a retirement account and you won't have to pay taxes or penalty. In general, it's a good idea to consolidate your retirement accounts as opposed to leaving them scattered in multiple places. If your previous employer's plan has poor investment options or charges high fees, rolling over to a new place will also give you better investment options and lower fees.

However, if your previous employer's plan is better than your new employer's plan, you can also choose to leave your money in the previous employer's plan. Make that a conscious choice as opposed to doing nothing. Make sure to keep your contact information updated with your previous employer's plan. You may be able to use your previous employer's plan as the place for consolidation because some plans still accept rollovers from former employees. For example, the Thrift Savings Plan (TSP) for federal government employees offers great investment options at very low cost. Former federal government employees can keep their TSP account open and roll over their 401(k) or 403(b) plan accounts to the TSP whenever they switch jobs.

Workplace retirement plans such as 401(k), 403(b), and TSP offer stronger protection against claims from creditors than IRAs in some states. If you're sued and you lose, the creditors can't take your money in workplace retirement plans as easily. If litigation risk is a concern for you, lean toward leaving the money in a workplace retirement plan as opposed to rolling over to an IRA.

Besides, if your income is high enough that makes you ineligible to contribute to a Roth IRA directly, leaving the money in a 401(k) or 403(b) plan will clear the way for making a "backdoor Roth" IRA contribution (see page 99).

After I left my former employer, I left the money in the employer's plan for some time when I still needed to do the "backdoor Roth." When I didn't need to do it anymore, I rolled the money over to a Traditional IRA.

Self-Employed

If you're self-employed, you're both the employer and the employee. You can set up a retirement plan for your business.

Solo 401(k)

If you don't have any employees other than your spouse, or if your employees don't ever work more than 1,000 hours a year, the best retirement plan for your business is a solo 401(k), also known as a *self-employed 401(k)* or an *individual 401(k)*. The solo 401(k) plan covers only yourself and your spouse (if he or she also works for the business). You can't use a solo 401(k) if you have employees who are over 21 and work 1,000 hours or more a year. I have a solo 401(k) plan for my self-employed business.

In a solo 401(k), as the *employee*, you can contribute up to the annual maximum as in a regular 401(k) plan ($19,500 in 2020, plus $6,500 for age 50 and over), in the same way as employees working for larger businesses do. In addition, you can contribute extra money as the *employer*. The limit is 25% of your salary if your business is taxed as an S-Corp or 20% of your net business profit if your business is taxed as a sole proprietor or partnership. When you contribute both as the employee and as the employer, if you have enough profit from your business, you can contribute as much as $57,000 total to your solo 401(k) in 2020.

The solo 401(k) can also be set up to have both Traditional pre-tax and Roth options. Remember my rule to favor Traditional over Roth. Investment companies such as Fidelity Investments, Charles Schwab, and Vanguard all offer a solo 401(k) plan. Fidelity and Charles Schwab only offer the Traditional pre-tax option. Vanguard offers both Traditional pre-tax and Roth options.

When the total assets in your solo 401(k) exceed $250,000, you need to file a Form 5500-EZ or Form 5500-SF annually with the government. This form isn't difficult to complete, but you must remember to file it. You also need to file it when you terminate the solo 401(k) plan, regardless of the size of the assets in the plan. If you're required to file the form but you don't, you'll face a steep penalty of $250 per day!

SEP-IRA

An alternative to a solo 401(k) is a SEP-IRA. You can choose either solo 401(k) or SEP-IRA, but not both for the same year. Many investment companies offer SEP-IRA accounts without maintenance fees.

You can only contribute to the SEP-IRA as the employer. As a result, your maximum contribution with a SEP-IRA is always less than or equal to your maximum contribution with a solo 401(k). If you have high self-employment income (say over $300,000 a year) such that the employer contributions alone will let you contribute the maximum $57,000 in 2020, going with a SEP-IRA is a little simpler than setting up a solo 401(k). If your self-employment income isn't as high, going with a solo 401(k) will let you contribute more.

Another disadvantage of using a SEP-IRA is that it will interfere with doing the "backdoor Roth" (see page 99). If you need to do the "backdoor Roth," consider using a solo 401(k), not a SEP-IRA.

If your business has employees other than your spouse who are over 21 and work 1,000 hours or more in a year, you can't use a solo 401(k) but you can still use a SEP-IRA. However, with a SEP-IRA, all employees must receive the same percentage of pay in employer contributions. A SIMPLE IRA (see below) would be a better choice in that case.

SIMPLE IRA

If you have employees who are over 21 and work at least 1,000 hours a year, the easiest plan is a SIMPLE IRA. You'll have to contribute 2% of payroll to all employees' accounts or 3% of pay as a matching contribution only to the employees who contribute themselves.

The downside of using a SIMPLE IRA for your business is that you can't contribute as much as you can in a full-fledged 401(k) plan. However, a full-fledged 401(k) plan costs more in administrative fees. If you'd like to explore setting up a full-fledged 401(k) plan for your business, consult a small business 401(k) provider such as Employee Fiduciary (employeefiduciary.com) or Guideline (guideline.com).

Other Plan Types

All my employers only offered a 401(k) plan. I mention these other types of plans in case you have them.

401(a) Plan

Some employers offer a 401(a) plan. There are two variations of 401(a) plans: mandatory pre-tax and voluntary after-tax.

In a mandatory pre-tax 401(a) plan, employees are required to contribute a set percentage of their pay to the plan. Sometimes the employee is given a choice in how much they'll contribute shortly after they start working for the employer, but the choice is one-time and irrevocable. Once the employee makes a choice, the choice can't be changed. The pre-tax contributions to the 401(a) plan don't count toward the elective deferral limit for 401(k) and 403(b) plans ($19,500 in 2020), but they do count toward the annual additions limit for all defined contribution plans at that employer ($57,000 in 2020).

A voluntary after-tax 401(a) plan is very much like the non-Roth after-tax contributions in a 401(k) or 403(b) plan (see page 81). Contributions are taken after-tax, but it's possible that the contributions and earnings can be rolled over to a Roth IRA via an in-service distribution to make it a "mega backdoor Roth" (see page 102).

457 Plan

Some government or non-profit employers offer a 457 plan. This can be in addition to a 401(k) or 403(b) plan. The contribution limit for a 457 plan is separate from the contribution limit for a 401(k) or 403(b) plan. For example, in 2020, you're allowed to contribute $19,500 to a 401(k) or 403(b) plan and another $19,500 to a 457 plan, doubling the maximum you can contribute otherwise.

If you work for a state or local government and you'd like to save more money for retirement, contribute to both a 401(k) or 403(b) plan and a 457 plan. Money in a non-governmental 457 plan is subject to claims from the employer's creditors. If you have a non-governmental 457 plan, consider your other options before jumping into the 457 plan.

A 457 plan can also offer both a Traditional pre-tax option and a Roth option. As in a 401(k) or 403(b) plan, favor Traditional over Roth by default.

SIMPLE IRA or SEP-IRA

Some smaller employers offer a *SIMPLE IRA* instead of a 401(k) or a 403(b) plan. They work similarly, except you have a lower contribution limit. The maximum contribution limit for a SIMPLE IRA is $13,500 in 2020, plus an additional $3,000 if you are 50 or over, as opposed to $19,500 and $6,500 respectively in a 401(k) or 403(b) plan.

If your employer offers a SIMPLE IRA, my rule is still the same: *contribute the maximum allowed.* Unlike a 401(k) or 403(b) plan where you're locked in until you leave the employer or reach age 59-1/2, you're allowed to roll over the money from your SIMPLE IRA to a personal IRA after you're in the plan for two years. In general, it's beneficial to do so.

Some smaller employers offer a *SEP-IRA.* As an employee, you don't get to contribute to it. You only receive contributions from the employer. You're free to move the money from the SEP-IRA to a personal IRA. In general, it's also beneficial to do so.

Pension Plan

Some employers, especially those in the public sector, still have a pension plan for their employees. These plans typically pay a percentage of pay for life after the employee works for the employer for a number of years and reaches a certain age. The greatest benefits are reserved for the long-tenured employees who stay with the employer until they retire. If you only work for the employer for a few years, you won't get much benefit from a pension plan.

As an employee, you don't have to do anything extra for the pension. You'll get credits for the pension just by working for the employer. The older you are, each additional year of working for the employer makes the pension worth more.

Some employers require the employees to contribute a certain percentage of their pay toward their pension. These required contributions don't count toward the contribution limits for your other plans.

Sometimes the employer will offer employees an opportunity to buy additional service years for the pension. You can do the math but these are almost always a sweet deal. The additional pension benefits are worth a lot more than the cash price.

Cash Balance Plan

Some employers offer a cash balance plan in lieu of a pension. The employer promises a sum of money based on a formula instead of a monthly pension benefit for life.

As an employee you also don't have to do anything extra for the benefits. The older you are, each additional year of working for the employer will also earn you more credits in the cash balance plan. The employer's contributions to the cash balance plan also don't count toward the contribution limits for your other plans.

Non-Qualified Deferred Compensation (NQDC) Plan

Some employers offer a Non-Qualified Deferred Compensation (NQDC) plan to managers above a certain level. If you're offered to participate, you can contribute a percentage of your pay pre-tax to the NQDC plan. The money can be invested in a menu of investment options, similar to in a 401(k) plan.

Contributions to the deferred compensation plan don't count toward the contribution limits for 401(k). You can contribute to both the 401(k) and the deferred compensation plan. When more contributions are taken pre-tax from your paychecks, you pay less in taxes.

The catch is that the money in the deferred compensation plan counts as the assets of the employer. It's subject to claims from the employer's creditors. You'll have to be comfortable with the financial health of your employer before you participate in the deferred compensation plan.

When you sign up for the deferred compensation plan, you choose how you'll receive the money when you leave the employer. You pay taxes when the money comes out of the plan. Some plans can spread the distribution over a number of years, which will lower the taxes you'll pay on the money, but you'll also have to trust the employer's financial health in those years.

Multiple Plans

If you participate in multiple plans, it can be confusing to figure out how the contribution limits work across all the plans. Remember these two limits: the *elective deferral limit* works on the employee across all employers, and the *annual additions limit* works on the employer across all plans at that specific employer. If you work for multiple unrelated employers, you get a separate annual additions limit at each employer. This handy table helps you figure out which limit applies to which types of contributions:

	Elective Deferral Limit	Annual Additions Limit
401(k)/403(b) Plan, pre-tax or Roth	Yes	Yes
Age 50 catch-up	No	No
401(k)/403(b) Plan, non-Roth after-tax	No	Yes
Employer contributions	No	Yes
457 Plan	No	No

	Elective Deferral Limit	Annual Additions Limit
401(a) Plan	No	Yes
SIMPLE IRA	Yes	Yes
SEP-IRA	No	Yes
Pension	No	No
Cash Balance Plan	No	No
Deferred Compensation	No	No

Example: Kate contributes $19,500 to her employer's 401(k) plan in 2020. Her employer contributes $4,500. The plan allows non-Roth after-tax contributions. She puts in another $33,000 as non-Roth after-tax contributions to fill up the $57,000 annual additions limit in 2020.

Kate also has a self-employment business on the side. She created a solo 401(k) plan for her business. She can't make Traditional pre-tax or Roth contributions to her solo 401(k) anymore because she already maxed out the elective deferral limit at her day job, but she can still contribute as the employer to her solo 401(k). She's not capped by the $57,000 contributions to her 401(k) at her day job because the $57,000 limit is *per employer* and her self-employed business is unrelated to her day job.

Chapter 6 Individual Retirement Accounts

In addition to participating in retirement plans at work, you can save for retirement on your own in an Individual Retirement Account (IRA). Some employers don't offer a retirement plan. In that case, it's even more important to save in an IRA. As in the previous chapter on workplace retirement plans, this chapter covers using the IRAs while Chapter 8 covers investing in these accounts.

The same primary rule in the previous chapter also applies to IRAs: *contribute the maximum allowed*. Which type of IRA to use and how you invest in your IRA are secondary to contributing the maximum in the first place. It's all moot without the contributions. Both my wife and I contributed the maximum to our IRAs every year since we realized we could save more for our retirement.

Traditional IRA

If you have compensation from working or self-employment, you can contribute to a Traditional IRA. If you don't work but your spouse does, and you file your taxes jointly, you're also eligible to contribute to a Traditional IRA. The Traditional IRA contribution may or may not be tax deductible, but you can always contribute as long as you have enough compensation income.

Contribution Limit

If you're not yet 50 years old, the annual contribution limit is $6,000 in 2020. It's $7,000 if you are 50 or older by the end of the year. This limit is separate from the contribution limit for 401(k) or 403(b). In 2020, you can contribute $19,500 to a 401(k) or 403(b) plan plus another $6,000 to an IRA. If you are 50 or older, you can contribute $26,000 to a 401(k) or 403(b) plan plus another $7,000 to an IRA.

The "I" in IRA stands for Individual. The account is only in one individual person's name. If you're married and both of you would like to contribute, you need to open separate accounts. The contribution limit applies to each person separately.

Income Limit

Contributions to a Traditional IRA can be tax deductible or non-deductible. Whether your contributions are deductible depends on your income, whether you're an active participant in a workplace retirement plan, and if you're married, whether your spouse is an active participant in a workplace retirement plan.

The income being measured is your Adjusted Gross Income on your tax return before any Traditional IRA contributions. If you already participate in a workplace retirement plan yourself, you have a lower income limit for taking a tax deduction on your contributions to a Traditional IRA. In 2020, the income limit for taking a full deduction is $65,000 for single and $104,000 for married filing jointly. You still get a partial deduction if your income is lower than $75,000 for single and $124,000 for married filing jointly.

If you're not an active participant in a workplace retirement plan and you're married but your spouse is, you have a higher income limit for taking a tax deduction on contributing to a Traditional IRA. In 2020, that income limit is $196,000 for married filing jointly. You still get a partial deduction if your income is lower than $206,000.

Finally, if you're not an active participant in a workplace retirement plan and you're single, or if you're married and your spouse isn't an active participant in a workplace retirement plan either, you can always take a tax deduction on your contributions to a Traditional IRA regardless of your income.

Therefore, based on your income, tax filing status, and your status of active participation in a workplace retirement plan, figure out whether you can take a tax deduction for contributing to a Traditional IRA. If you can, open a Traditional IRA at an investment company such as Vanguard, Fidelity Investments, or Charles Schwab, and make the contribution.

Example: Tom and Jackie are married and they file a joint tax return. Tom has a 401(k) plan at work but Jackie doesn't. Their joint adjusted gross income is $140,000. Because this is higher than $124,000, Tom, as an active participant in a workplace retirement plan, won't get a tax deduction if he contributes to a Traditional IRA. However, because Jackie isn't an active participant in a workplace retirement plan and their joint income is lower than the $196,000 limit, Jackie will get a full tax deduction when she contributes to a Traditional IRA.

If you can't take a tax deduction, check the next sections to see if you can contribute to a Roth IRA or whether you must do a "backdoor Roth."

Contribution Deadline

Although you can wait until April 15 of the following year to contribute for the previous year, it's best to contribute early. Your money will have more time to grow inside the IRA. If you're only able to make a non-deductible contribution to a Traditional IRA, contributing for the current year as opposed to waiting until the following year will also make your tax reporting much easier.

Receive Rollovers

Due to the income limit, many people who have a 401(k) or 403(b) plan at work can't take a tax deduction for contributing to a

Traditional IRA. However, you can still open a Traditional IRA only for receiving rollovers from a workplace retirement plan when you switch jobs (see page 83). Moving your money from a Traditional 401(k) or 403(b) into a Traditional IRA preserves the money's pre-tax status.

It's a convenient way to consolidate your retirement savings into one place. It also gives you more control over the investment options. According to a study by researchers at Boston College, most people have a Traditional IRA not from making direct contributions but from using it as the destination for rollovers.

Roth IRA

Roth IRA is an alternative to Traditional IRA. Contributions to a Roth IRA aren't tax deductible, but eligible withdrawals from a Roth IRA are tax-free. Roth IRA also adds some flexibility in that you can withdraw the original contributions at any time tax-free without any penalty, even before age 59-1/2.

While you can contribute to both a Traditional IRA and a Roth IRA for the same year, the contribution limit is shared between these two types of IRAs. The contributions to both Traditional IRA and Roth IRA added together can't exceed the annual contribution limit. If your annual limit is $6,000 because you're not yet 50, you can contribute all $6,000 to a Traditional IRA and zero to a Roth IRA, or you can contribute zero to a Traditional IRA and $6,000 to a Roth IRA, or half-and-half, or any other combination.

In the previous chapter, we covered why you should by default favor Traditional over Roth in workplace retirement plans (see page 79). The same reasoning applies to the IRA as well. Unless you know your income will increase dramatically in the future, contribute to a Roth IRA only when you can't take a tax deduction for contributing to a Traditional IRA.

Income Limit

Even though the Roth IRA contributions aren't tax deductible, the law still sets an income limit for contributing to a Roth IRA. The income limit for Roth IRA is higher than the income limit for taking a deduction on Traditional IRA contributions. As a result, there is a range of income where you can't take a deduction for contributing to a Traditional IRA but you can contribute to a Roth IRA.

In 2020, if your tax filing status is single, the income limit for making a full contribution to a Roth IRA is $124,000. The limit is $196,000 for married filing jointly. You get a partial contribution if your income is under $139,000 for single and $206,000 for married filing jointly. If your income is higher yet, you're not allowed to contribute to a Roth IRA directly.

In our previous example, Tom and Jackie are married filing jointly with $140,000 in adjusted gross income. Tom, as an active participant in a workplace retirement plan, won't get a tax deduction if he contributes to a Traditional IRA, but he can still contribute to a Roth IRA. If their joint income is $240,000 instead of $140,000, neither of them can contribute to a Roth IRA.

The income limit for married filing separately is only $10,000. If you must file separately, it pretty much eliminates your ability to contribute to a Roth IRA. In that case, if your income doesn't qualify for a deduction on a Traditional IRA contribution, the "backdoor Roth" (see page 99) is your only option.

Recharacterization

Due to the income limit, and because you can never be sure what your income will be until you file your taxes, the IRS allows you to change your contribution type after the fact. This is called *recharacterizing* your IRA contribution.

Example: Jane, single, contributes to her 401(k) plan at work. She also contributed to her Traditional IRA thinking she would get a tax deduction. Her adjusted gross income turned out to be $80,000, which exceeded the income limit for making a deductible contribution to the Traditional IRA. Because her income is still below the income limit for making a Roth IRA contribution, she can recharacterize her Traditional IRA contribution as a Roth IRA contribution.

Example: Mike is married filing jointly with his wife. They both contribute to 401(k) plans at work. They also contributed to their Roth IRAs. When they prepare their taxes, the tax software told them their income exceeded the limit for making Roth IRA contributions. They are able to recharacterize their Roth IRA contributions as Traditional IRA contributions.

The financial institutions all have special procedures for recharacterizing IRA contributions. When you fill out the paperwork to recharacterize, they'll follow the IRS rules to calculate how much money needs to move from one type of IRA to the other. After they move the money, it's as if you contributed to the other IRA type from the beginning.

If you need to recharacterize your contribution, you have to do it before the tax filing deadline, including extension. After the deadline passes, you can't recharacterize anymore.

Roth Conversion

You're also allowed to transfer money from your Traditional IRA to your Roth IRA. This is called a Roth *conversion*. It affects the money already in the Traditional IRA. It doesn't change the type of your IRA contributions.

Anyone can convert an unlimited amount at any time. The catch is that you have to pay taxes on the pre-tax money converted to the Roth IRA. For this reason, it's better to convert only when you are in a low tax bracket. If you're in a high tax bracket, you should avoid converting substantial pre-tax money, and only convert after-tax money (see "backdoor Roth" in the next section). Wait until you retire in a lower tax bracket or during a career break when your tax bracket is temporarily low before you convert substantial pre-tax money.

"Backdoor Roth"

A maneuver unofficially referred to as the "backdoor Roth" also uses a Roth conversion. It allows you to put money into a Roth IRA indirectly when your income is too high such that you can't take a tax deduction for contributing to a Traditional IRA and you can't contribute to a Roth IRA either. If your income allows you to take a tax deduction on a Traditional IRA contribution, you would just contribute to a Traditional IRA. If your income allows you to contribute to a Roth IRA, you would just contribute to a Roth IRA. When your income is too high to do either, the "backdoor Roth" is your only option.

Because you can still *contribute* to a Traditional IRA at any income (the income limit for Traditional IRA is only for taking a tax deduction), and you can *convert* from a Traditional IRA to a Roth IRA at any time without restriction, when you combine the two steps together, money ends up in your Roth IRA indirectly.

A "backdoor Roth" is performed this way:
1. Make a non-deductible contribution to a Traditional IRA;
2. Transfer the money from the Traditional IRA to a Roth IRA (i.e. convert to Roth IRA).

Normally when you do a Roth conversion, you'll pay taxes on the money transferred from the Traditional IRA to the Roth IRA. However, in a "backdoor Roth," because the Traditional IRA contribution is non-deductible, you don't pay taxes again when you transfer the after-tax money to the Roth IRA. You only pay taxes on any earnings on the money while it stayed in the Traditional IRA. If the money doesn't stay in the Traditional IRA for long, the earnings will be minimal.

Pro-Rata Rule

The IRS sees all Traditional IRAs, SEP-IRAs, and SIMPLE IRAs under one person's name as one large Traditional IRA, regardless of how many actual accounts you have with different financial institutions. When you have both pre-tax and post-tax money in your Traditional IRAs, SEP-IRAs, and SIMPLE IRAs, your Roth conversion is considered as coming from both pre-tax and post-tax money proportionally ("pro rata" in Latin), regardless of which actual account you use for the conversion.

As a result, if you have $194,000 in a Traditional IRA from a rollover from a previous employer's 401(k) plan, and you make a $6,000 non-deductible contribution to a new Traditional IRA, in the eyes of the IRS, you have one big Traditional IRA with $200,000, 3% of which is after-tax money. When you convert $6,000 to Roth, even if you specifically use the $6,000 you just contributed, it's still considered as 97% pre-tax and 3% post-tax, and you'll pay taxes on 97% of the $6,000.

To get around this pro-rata rule, you can't have substantial pre-tax money in any Traditional IRA, SEP-IRA, or SIMPLE IRA (inherited IRAs don't count) at the end of the year when you do the "backdoor Roth." You also can't roll over substantial pre-tax money to a Traditional IRA in the same year after you do the "backdoor Roth." If you already have substantial pre-tax money in a Traditional

IRA from rollovers of previous workplace retirement plans, the pre-tax money can be rolled back into a workplace retirement plan. Most 401(k) and 403(b) plans accept rollovers from IRAs. If you're self-employed, the pre-tax IRA money can be rolled over into a solo 401(k) plan (except Vanguard's solo 401(k) plan doesn't allow it). Pre-tax money in a workplace retirement plan or a solo 401(k) plan isn't included in the pro-rata rule.

The pro-rata rule is applied to each person individually, because IRAs are only under one person's name. If you're married, your Traditional IRAs and your spouse's Traditional IRAs are separate. One person having pre-tax money in Traditional IRAs doesn't affect the other person's calculation. It's possible that one person has to clear the way for a "backdoor Roth" but the other person doesn't.

Example: Lisa's income is too high for contributing to a Roth IRA. She doesn't have any other Traditional IRAs, SEP-IRAs, or SIMPLE IRAs. She opens a Traditional IRA and makes a non-deductible contribution before she transfers the money from the Traditional IRA to a Roth IRA. She pays taxes on the small amount of earnings in the Traditional IRA. She also makes sure she keeps her 401(k) money in a 401(k) plan. She doesn't roll over her 401(k) account to a Traditional IRA when she switches jobs.

Example: Phil and Cindy's joint income is too high for contributing to a Roth IRA. Cindy doesn't have any Traditional IRAs, SEP-IRAs, or SIMPLE IRAs. She does the "backdoor Roth" in the same way as Lisa in the previous example. Phil has a Traditional IRA with money from 401(k) rollovers from his previous jobs. In order to do the "backdoor Roth," Phil first moves the Traditional IRA money back into his current 401(k) plan at work. He then makes a non-deductible contribution to the Traditional IRA, followed by transferring the money to a Roth IRA. Phil also makes sure he keeps his 401(k) money in a 401(k) plan. He doesn't roll over his 401(k) account to a Traditional IRA when he switches jobs.

Form 8606

When you do a "backdoor Roth," you're required to include a Form 8606 with your tax return. If you're married, and both of you did a "backdoor Roth," you'll need to include two separate copies of Form 8606. If you e-file with tax software, do a preview of the forms before you file. If it doesn't include a Form 8606, it means you didn't answer the questions correctly in the software.

Because the questions in tax software can be confusing, it's best to keep the two steps in a "backdoor Roth" maneuver in the same calendar year. Make a contribution for 2020 in 2020 and complete the conversion in 2020. If you make the contribution for 2020 in 2021 and do the conversion in 2021, because the contribution is for the previous year, you'll be more confused when you file your taxes. If you're already behind, contribute for both the previous year and the current year and convert the total at the same time. For example, you contribute $6,000 for 2019 before April 15, 2020, plus another $6,000 for 2020, before you convert total $12,000 in 2020. Then in 2021 you'll contribute for 2021 and convert in 2021.

I have detailed walkthroughs for how to answer the questions for "backdoor Roth" in different tax software on my blog. Please see Appendix for links.

"Mega Backdoor Roth"

A "mega backdoor Roth" (see page 81) involves making non-Roth after-tax contributions to a workplace retirement plan, followed by transferring the money to the Roth account within the 401(k) plan via an *In-plan Roth Rollover* or by moving the money to a Roth IRA via an *In-Service Distribution*. It requires a workplace retirement plan that allows non-Roth after-tax contributions and either In-Plan Roth Rollovers or In-Service Distributions.

Transferring to the Roth account within the plan is more convenient because the money stays in the plan. Moving the money to a Roth IRA gives you more control over the investment options. If you decide to use a Roth IRA as the destination for your "mega backdoor Roth," make sure the rollover from your workplace retirement plan goes straight to the Roth IRA. When the money goes from the workplace retirement plan directly to a Roth IRA, it's not subject to the pro-rata rule (see page 100). It still works even if you already have a Traditional IRA, SEP-IRA, or SIMPLE IRA with pre-tax money. If the money first goes into a Traditional IRA, then it'll be subject to the pro-rata rule.

Chapter 7 Saving for College

Many parents save and invest for their kids' college education expenses. The best vehicle for a college savings fund is a 529 plan.

There are two types of 529 plans: *529 prepaid plans* and *529 savings plans*. The 529 prepaid plans are tied to tuition rates at public universities within a specific state. The 529 savings plans are more flexible. The student can go to any accredited college in the country. This chapter only covers 529 savings plans.

529 Savings Plan

A 529 savings plan works like a Roth IRA in that you put in after-tax money but the earnings are tax-free when the money is used for qualified education expenses. If you save the money outside a 529 plan, the interest, dividends, and capital gains will be taxed.

Suppose you contribute $1,000 every year to a 529 plan for a child, and you earn a 5% return in the 529 plan. In 18 years, the $18,000 you put in will grow to close to $30,000. When you use the $30,000 in the 529 plan for college expenses, the $12,000 growth is tax-free. If you don't use a 529 plan and you put the money in a regular account, you'll have to pay taxes on the dividends and interest during the 18 years, and you'll have to pay taxes on the appreciation when you sell your investments.

Owner and Beneficiary

As the adult owner of the 529 plan account, you designate a person as the beneficiary. The beneficiary must be a U.S. citizen or resident. The beneficiary can be your child, your grandchild, your nephew or niece, or even yourself or another adult. When you own the account and designate your child as the beneficiary, your extended family members can contribute to it for your child as well. You can have multiple separate accounts for different beneficiaries. If you have plans to go to graduate school or professional school (MBA, law school, etc.) in the future, you can use the 529 plan and designate yourself as the beneficiary.

If the beneficiary of a 529 plan account does not go to college, receives a scholarship, or otherwise doesn't need all the money in the account, you can change the beneficiary on the account to an eligible family member of the original beneficiary. The most common change would be if one child doesn't need all the money, you change the beneficiary to another child. If you run out of beneficiaries to change to and you still have excess money in the account, when you take the money out, the portion attributed to the original contributions isn't taxed, however the earnings portion may be taxed and subject to a 10% penalty.

Contribution Limits

The IRS considers contributions to a 529 plan account as a gift to the beneficiary. In 2020, each adult can give up to $15,000 to any one person without having to file a gift tax return. If you have several children, you can contribute up to $15,000 a year to each child's 529 plan account.

If you'd like to fund the accounts up front, you can also contribute five years' worth of gifts ($75,000 in 2020) in one year and skip the next four years. This is called *superfunding* a 529 plan account. If you choose superfunding, you do have to file a gift tax return (Form 709) but the amount does not affect your estate tax exemption.

Money in a 529 plan account counts as the owner's (typically a parent's) assets in the financial aid qualification. It has a lower impact on financial aid than money in the student's name. Money taken out of a 529 plan account owned by a grandparent counts as the student's income in the financial aid qualification. Many grandparents wait and pay out of their 529 plan accounts after the money is no longer counted in the final year's financial aid application.

State Income Tax Benefits

529 plans are sponsored by the states. Each state has a different 529 plan. Some states have multiple 529 plans. Most plans accept both in-state and out-of-state residents. Money in one state's 529 savings plan isn't limited to covering college expenses within that state. As a result, when you open a 529 plan account, you can choose to use a 529 plan from your home state or you can choose a 529 plan from a different state. If you started with one 529 plan, you can roll over to another 529 plan if you like the other plan better now. You can even choose to use multiple 529 plans at the same time.

Whether you should choose a 529 plan from your home state or from a different state depends on what tax benefits your state gives you and how good the investment options in your home state's 529 plans are.

Some states give their taxpayers state income tax benefits for contributing to a 529 plan. The state income tax benefits usually come in the form of a tax deduction up to a certain amount (a handful of states have no cap). The state tax benefits may be limited to the contributions only to a home-state 529 plan or they may be given for contributing to *any* 529 plan. For example, the state of Indiana gives a 20% tax credit of up to $1,000 a year. If you're an Indiana taxpayer and you contribute $5,000, you'll get $1,000 tax credit from Indiana. But this benefit is limited to only Indiana taxpayers and only for contributing to Indiana's 529 plan. On the other hand, the state of Montana makes 529 plan contributions tax deductible for its residents (up to a certain amount each year), and it doesn't matter which state's 529 plan the contributions go into.

Therefore, when you choose a 529 plan, you should first find out whether your home state offers any state income tax benefits for contributing, and whether the benefits are limited to only a home-state plan.

"Go Anywhere" States

Some states don't offer any tax benefits for contributing to a 529 plan. My state, California, is one of them. I still get the tax-free earnings but I don't get any additional incentive from the state for making the contributions. Some states don't have a state income tax. They don't have any extra incentive to give when the tax rate is already zero. Washington, Nevada, Texas, Florida, and a few other states are like that. Some states offer tax benefits but they don't limit the benefits to only a home-state plan (as in the Montana example). In all these cases, you can choose any 529 plan in the country. It doesn't make any difference in terms of state tax benefits – either you don't get any state tax benefits anyway or you always get the state tax benefits.

By my research, the following 22 states are in this "go anywhere" category:

Alaska	Arizona	California
Delaware	Florida	Hawaii
Kansas	Kentucky	Maine
Minnesota	Missouri	Montana
Nevada	New Hampshire	New Jersey
North Carolina	Pennsylvania	South Dakota
Tennessee	Texas	Washington
Wyoming		

When you live in one of these "go anywhere" states, you can go for the best 529 plan in the country (see page 110).

"Deduct and Run" States

Some states limit the state tax benefits to only contributions to their own 529 plan, but they don't take back the state tax benefits if you decide to do a rollover from a home-state 529 plan to an out-of-state 529 plan at a later time. If you want the state tax benefits, you'll have to contribute to a home-state 529 plan. If you think the home-state plan is good enough, you can choose to stay. If you really like a 529 plan sponsored by a different state better than the one from your home state, you can choose to contribute to the home-state plan first, get the state tax benefits, and then roll over the money to the 529 plan you really want. I call this "deduct and run."

By my research, the following 13 states plus Washington, DC allow "deduct and run":

- Connecticut
- District of Columbia (after two years)
- Louisiana
- Maryland
- Massachusetts
- Michigan
- Mississippi
- North Dakota
- Oklahoma (after one year)
- Oregon
- Rhode Island (after two years)
- South Carolina
- Vermont
- West Virginia

However, we should keep the benefits of "deduct and run" in perspective. If you contribute $3,000 a year and the state income tax rate is 5%, a $3,000 tax deduction on your state income tax return is worth $150 a year. If you really like a different 529 plan, you may choose to forego the $150 in state tax benefits and go directly to the plan you really like. If the home-state 529 plan isn't that bad, choosing to stay and avoid the hassle of moving to a different plan would be perfectly valid as well.

Incentivized States

Finally, by my research, these remaining 15 states limit the state tax benefits to only the home-state 529 plans, and they'll take back the state tax benefits if you do a rollover to an out-of-state 529 plan. They offer an incentive for their taxpayers to use the home-state 529 plans.

Alabama	Arkansas	Colorado
Georgia	Idaho	Illinois
Indiana	Iowa	Nebraska
New Mexico	New York	Ohio
Utah	Virginia	Wisconsin

If you live in these states, you should consider the state tax benefits and the quality of the home-state plan. If the home-state plan is quite good, you might as well contribute to the home-state plan and receive the state tax benefits. If the state tax benefits aren't that much and the home-state plan isn't that good, you may choose to forego the state tax benefits for a better plan elsewhere.

Also remember state laws can and do change. Before you decide to go one way or another, double-check the current tax benefits from your state.

The Best 529 Plans

Each 529 plan has a different menu of investment options. Some plans have better investment options than others. Investment research company Morningstar (morningstar.com) rates 529 plans in the country. They consider only the quality of the investment options, not the state tax benefits.

The following plans received a Gold rating from Morningstar in 2019:

- Illinois Bright Start College Savings Plan
- Virginia Invest529 Plan
- Utah my529 Plan
- California ScholarShare College Savings Plan

If you live in one of the "go anywhere" states, consider using one of these Gold-rated plans. If you live in other states, check the Morningstar rating of your home-state plan. If it's still rated Silver, maybe it's worth staying put in the home-state plan. If it's rated Bronze, Neutral, or not rated, see whether your state tax benefits are enough to keep you from going to one of the Gold-rated plans.

I contribute to a 529 plan account for my niece. My niece's 529 plan account is with Ohio CollegeAdvantage Direct 529 Savings Plan. It's rated as Silver by Morningstar. Although one of the Gold-rated plans may be better, it's still "good enough." The difference isn't large enough to make it worth moving at this point.

Rollover

If you move from one state to another, or if you like another state's 529 plan better, you can do a rollover from one state's plan to another state's plan. Some states give state tax benefits to rollover contributions too. You can do a rollover for each beneficiary once every rolling one-year period.

The owner and the beneficiary don't change in the rollover. You open a new account with the same owner and the same beneficiary at the new plan. Then you fill out a rollover form from the new plan. The new plan will contact your current plan to have the money transferred. The old plan will tell the new plan how much of the money is from contributions and how much of it is earnings. The new plan will continue the accounting.

Distributions

When you take money out of a 529 plan account to pay for the beneficiary's qualified education expenses, the distribution is tax-free. Qualified expenses include both tuition and fees. If the student is enrolled at least half-time, qualified expenses also include the college's allowance for room and board.

A recent federal law also included up to $10,000 a year in K-12 tuition and fees as qualified education expenses, but not all states followed this change in the federal law. If you withdraw for K-12 tuition and fees, the money is exempt from federal income tax but your state may still tax it.

You must match the withdrawals with qualified expenses paid on a calendar year basis. If you're paying a tuition bill in January, don't withdraw in the previous December. If you paid a bill in December, don't wait until the next January to do the withdrawal, because it won't have matching expenses in the same calendar year.

If your income qualifies for a tax credit or a tax deduction for higher education expenses, such as the American Opportunity Tax Credit (AOTC), the Lifetime Learning Tax Credit, or the Tuition and Fees deduction, the expenses used to qualify for the tax credit or the tax deduction must not be paid from a 529 plan – no double-dipping. If you'd like to get the tax credit or the tax deduction, pay the required expenses out of pocket, and pay the remainder from the 529 plan.

Chapter 8 Investing

When you put money into a retirement plan, an IRA, an HSA, or a 529 plan, you can invest the money for long-term growth. Investing is important, but it's not as important as contributing the money to invest in the first place. The financial industry and the media make investing appear very complicated. It's not.

What Investing Is About

Knowing what investing *isn't* about will help you see clearly what investing really *is* about. On a random day, I saw these headlines on a major financial media website:

- *"The last time this 'clear danger sign' flashed in the stock market was in 1999, and we all know what happened next"*
- *"What interest rates dating back to 1311 tell us about today's global economy"*
- *"Goldman Sachs: These 2 Stocks Are Poised to Surge by at Least 20%"*
- *"Tesla stock could hit $6,000 per share in the next five years, analyst says"*

The headlines give the impression that investing is about figuring out what the markets will do next or which investments will do really well. They are absolutely correct in that it's really helpful *if* you can figure out what the markets will do next or which investments will do well. The problem is the big "if."

No Market Timing, No Stock Picking

If you can tell the market will continue going up, you would stay in the market and continue buying. When you see the market is about to go down, you sell and wait until the storm passes. After you see the market has reached the bottom, you buy back in. Buy low, sell high. Rinse and repeat. You'll ride with the market on the way up and you'll step to the side on the way down. This strategy is called *market timing*. You buy or sell based on where you see the market is going.

If you know which two stocks will surge by at least 20% shortly, you would buy those two stocks. After they surge, you sell for a big profit and you find the next two stocks that are poised to surge. If Tesla stock will hit $6,000 per share in the next five years (from $500 per share when I saw the headline), of course you should buy Tesla stock and see it hit $6,000 per share in five years. This strategy is called *stock picking*. There are always individual stocks that do better than the overall market. If you pick those winners you'll have great returns.

The problem with market timing and stock picking strategies is that so many people are trying to do the same thing and they spend much more time and money on the pursuit than you and I can ever dream of. By definition, if you time the market well, or if you pick the right stocks, you'll do well. When a lot of money is on the line, people go to extreme lengths to achieve such success. Wall Street firms employ teams of Ph.D.'s and powerful computers. They grind tons of data to try to figure out which way the market is going or which stocks will do better. If it's obvious the market will go up, money will come in and push up the prices to a point where it's not so obvious the market will still go up. If it's obvious the market will go down, they will sell and pull down the prices to a point where it's not so obvious the market will still go down. If it's obvious Tesla stock will hit $6,000 per share in the next five years, the price won't be left at $500 per share today.

If someone can reliably tell which way the market is going or which stocks will do well, their skills are in great demand by Wall Street. They aren't going to tell us for free. Any analysis we mere mortals see is just unreliable speculation. Some of them will be correct, but they will be correct only by dumb luck.

Index Funds and ETFs Over Active Managers

"If you can't beat them, join them."

It's not just us small time retail investors who can't tell which way the market is going or which stocks will do well. Many highly paid professional fund managers can't either.

Mutual funds gather money from investors into a pool. They hire professional managers to buy and sell investments in the pool. Attempting to beat the market through buying and selling is called active management. Funds that take this approach are called *actively managed funds.*

After the professional managers and their analysts in actively managed funds apply their expertise, experience, and research, the vast majority of them still can't beat the market. S&P Dow Jones Indices LLC tracks the performance of actively managed funds in their SPIVA Scorecard reports. The latest data showed that, for the 15-year period ended June 30, 2019, 88% of all U.S. equity funds did not beat the market, and 90% of all international equity funds did not beat the market. These professional fund managers can't beat the market because the market itself is the result of all professional investors' activities. When professional fund managers buy and sell, they are competing against equally knowledgeable and experienced professional investors. The professional fund managers who succeed in one period tend to fall behind in subsequent periods.

It's tempting to think that if only we pay more attention and do more research, we will be able to see things others don't, or if only we hire the right professional managers, they'll be able to do better than the markets. I'd been down those paths. I read. I researched. I invested in funds run by award-winning managers. It didn't work until I found the right approach in simply investing in broadly diversified index funds and Exchange Traded Funds (ETFs).

Broadly diversified index funds and ETFs don't attempt to predict which way the market is going or which stocks or bonds will do better than the market. They only match their respective markets by investing in practically every stock and every bond in the market. By giving up the dream of beating the market, they end up beating the vast majority of professional fund managers. There's a saying "If you can't beat them, join them." That's the approach of investing in broadly diversified index funds and ETFs.

Low cost plays a big role in the success of broadly diversified index funds and ETFs. They charge very low fees because they don't attempt to beat the market. The annual fees charged by mutual funds and ETFs are called the *expense ratio*. The expense ratios of the broadly diversified index funds and ETFs I invest in are below 0.1%, which means I pay less than $1 per year for every $1,000 I invest. Expense ratios of actively managed funds are much higher. Some actively managed funds charge well over 1%, which means you pay 10 or 15 times more for investing in actively managed funds and you often end up with worse results.

Although both 0.1% and 1% look like small numbers, paying 1% versus 0.1% makes a big difference over one's lifetime. If you invest $10,000 a year for 40 years, and you pay 1% a year versus 0.1% a year, you'll have 20% less at the end of 40 years.

Target Date Funds

A *target date fund* is a mutual fund designed for people who plan to retire around a target year. It invests in a professionally selected mix of other funds. It automatically rebalances when some funds in the mix perform better than others (see page 131). It also automatically adjusts the mix as time moves closer to the target year.

A target date fund typically has the target year in its name. For example, these funds are target date funds designed for people who plan to retire around the year 2030:

- Vanguard Target Retirement 2030 Fund
- Fidelity Freedom Index 2030 Fund
- Schwab Target 2030 Index Fund

The same fund series also have funds for people who plan to retire around 2025, 2035, 2040, etc. The idea is that you pick just one fund by the target year closest to when you plan to retire.

Suppose you choose the Vanguard Target Retirement 2030 Fund. This fund invests in these four underlying funds:

- Vanguard Total Stock Market Index Fund
- Vanguard Total International Stock Index Fund
- Vanguard Total Bond Market II Index Fund
- Vanguard Total International Bond Index Fund

The first fund, Vanguard Total Stock Market Index Fund, invests in 3,500 stocks in the U.S. The second fund, Vanguard Total International Stock Index Fund, invests in 7,400 stocks outside the U.S. The third fund, Vanguard Total Bond Market II Index Fund, invests in 9,000 bonds in the U.S. The fourth fund, Vanguard Total International Bond Index, invests in 6,000 bonds outside the U.S. Now, by investing in just one target date fund, you're investing in over 10,000 stocks and over 15,000 bonds, both in the U.S. and outside the U.S. That's broadly diversified. When the fund automatically manages the mix, you achieve "set and forget." All you have to do is put money into this one fund.

Target date funds are a great choice for investing in a workplace retirement plan or an IRA. I like this quote I read on an investing forum:

"If you're not sure whether a target date fund is a good choice for you, it's a good a choice for you."

Many 401(k) plans offer a series of target date funds. You can also buy a target date fund in your IRA or HSA. If you're not sure how to invest, simply choosing a target date fund is a great solution.

A target date fund costs slightly more than buying its components directly. For example, Vanguard Target Retirement 2030 Fund charges 0.14% per year for investing in a mix of four underlying funds. If you buy the four underlying funds directly and you mix them on your own, you'll pay a weighted average of 0.07% per year. You can think of the extra 0.07% per year as an overhead cost for managing the mix.

By mixing different investments together in one fund, a target date fund minimizes the distraction when one component does well and another component does poorly. If you buy four funds separately and you see that one fund did poorly, you may second-guess and wonder whether you should make a shift. The shift you end up making tends to happen at the worst time, when you can't take it anymore.

You're less prone to tinkering with your investments when you invest in just one target date fund. Whichever way the wind blows, your target year hasn't changed. Therefore that same target date fund is still your choice. This behavioral benefit can be worth much more than the slight overhead cost in a target date fund over buying its components directly and mixing on your own.

Target Date Index Funds

A target date fund invests in other funds. Those other funds can be index funds or actively managed funds. If you have a choice, choose a target date fund that invests in index funds.

Vanguard's target date funds, called Vanguard Target Retirement Funds, all invest in index funds. Fidelity Investments and Charles Schwab offer two series of target date funds. One series invest in index funds and the other series invest in actively managed funds. The fund that invests in index funds has the word "Index" in it. For example, Fidelity Freedom *Index* 2030 Fund invests in index funds, and Fidelity Freedom 2030 Fund (without the word "Index") invests in actively managed funds. Schwab Target 2030 *Index* Fund invests in index funds, and Schwab Target 2030 Fund (without the word "Index") invests in actively managed funds.

Your workplace retirement plan may have chosen only the series that invest in actively managed funds. When you're able to choose in your IRA or HSA, you want a target date fund that invests in index funds.

Vanguard, Fidelity, Charles Schwab

Vanguard (investor.vanguard.com), Fidelity Investments (fidelity.com), and Charles Schwab (schwab.com) are the "big 3" investment companies for retail investors. They all offer Traditional IRA, Roth IRA, and regular taxable investment accounts with no maintenance fees. They all have target date index funds. I have accounts with Vanguard and Fidelity. I would be comfortable using Charles Schwab as well. All three companies are good choices.

Vanguard offers these target date index funds:

- Vanguard Target Retirement Income Fund (VTINX)
- Vanguard Target Retirement 2015 Fund (VTXVX)
- Vanguard Target Retirement 2020 Fund (VTWNX)
- Vanguard Target Retirement 2025 Fund (VTTVX)
- Vanguard Target Retirement 2030 Fund (VTHRX)
- Vanguard Target Retirement 2035 Fund (VTTHX)
- Vanguard Target Retirement 2040 Fund (VFORX)
- Vanguard Target Retirement 2045 Fund (VTIVX)
- Vanguard Target Retirement 2050 Fund (VFIFX)
- Vanguard Target Retirement 2055 Fund (VFFVX)
- Vanguard Target Retirement 2060 Fund (VTTSX)
- Vanguard Target Retirement 2065 Fund (VLXVX)

Vanguard Target Retirement Income Fund (VTINX) is for retirees. The other funds in the list are for people who will retire around the respective years in the fund names.

Fidelity Investments offers these following target date index funds:

- Fidelity Freedom Index 2005 Fund (FJIFX)
- Fidelity Freedom Index 2010 Fund (FKIFX)
- Fidelity Freedom Index 2015 Fund (FLIFX)
- Fidelity Freedom Index 2020 Fund (FPIFX)
- Fidelity Freedom Index 2025 Fund (FQIFX)
- Fidelity Freedom Index 2030 Fund (FXIFX)
- Fidelity Freedom Index 2035 Fund (FIHFX)
- Fidelity Freedom Index 2040 Fund (FBIFX)
- Fidelity Freedom Index 2045 Fund (FIOFX)
- Fidelity Freedom Index 2050 Fund (FIPFX)
- Fidelity Freedom Index 2055 Fund (FDEWX)
- Fidelity Freedom Index 2060 Fund (FDKLX)

Charles Schwab offers these target date index funds:

- Schwab Target 2010 Index Fund (SWYAX)
- Schwab Target 2015 Index Fund (SWYBX)
- Schwab Target 2020 Index Fund (SWYLX)
- Schwab Target 2025 Index Fund (SWYDX)
- Schwab Target 2030 Index Fund (SWYEX)
- Schwab Target 2035 Index Fund (SWYFX)
- Schwab Target 2040 Index Fund (SWYGX)
- Schwab Target 2045 Index Fund (SWYHX)
- Schwab Target 2050 Index Fund (SWYMX)
- Schwab Target 2055 Index Fund (SWYJX)
- Schwab Target 2060 Index Fund (SWYNX)

Age-Based Portfolio in 529 Plans

Many 529 plans offer age-based portfolio options. Similar to target date funds in retirement accounts, an age-based portfolio invests in a professionally selected mix of other funds, and it automatically adjusts the mix by the beneficiary's age. When the child is young, the age-based portfolio invests more in stock funds. When the child gets closer to attending college, the age-based portfolio invests more in fixed-income funds.

An age-based portfolio option is a great choice in a 529 plan. It allows you to focus on what really matters: your contributions. Similar to target date funds, when you're not sure whether the age-based portfolio is a good choice for you in a 529 plan, it's a good choice for you.

Also similar to target date funds, some age-based portfolio options invest in index funds, and some age-based portfolio options invest in actively managed funds. Some 529 plans offer both tracks.

In that case, you want the track that invests in index funds. Sometimes it's called the "passive" option.

For example, California's ScholarShare 529 plan offers a Passive Age-Based Investment Portfolio together with an Active Age-Based Investment Portfolio. The Passive Age-Based Investment Portfolio invests in index funds while the Active Age-Based Investment Portfolio invests in actively managed funds. I would choose the Passive Age-Based Investment Portfolio in this plan.

Besides the word *Index* or *Passive*, you can also tell by the fees charged. The total fees of the Passive Age-Based Investment Portfolio in the California ScholarShare 529 plan range from 0.08% per year to 0.12% per year. The total fees of the Active Age-Based Investment Portfolio range from 0.28% per year to 0.52% per year. The fees are about four times as high in the Active Age-Based Investment Portfolio.

Just to repeat, when you pick an age-based portfolio in a 529 plan, be sure to pick one that invests in index funds.

3-Fund Portfolio

If your workplace retirement plan doesn't offer target date funds, or if the target date funds in the plan menu only invest in actively managed funds, you may be able to create a simple but highly effective asset allocation on your own.

Asset allocation means how you put your investments together to form a diversified and balanced portfolio. You should have some stocks and some fixed-income investments. You should have some U.S. stocks and some international stocks. Just having these three major components will cover your bases:

- U.S. stocks
- International stocks
- High-quality fixed-income investments

Answer Two Questions

When you build a 3-fund portfolio, you come up with the percentages for each component by answering these two questions:

---

1. How much in stocks?

2. Among stocks, how much in international?

That's it. You don't have to make it any more complicated than that.

A good starting point to answer the first question would be to copy the expert recommendations based on how soon you'll retire, such as these (adapted from what Vanguard chose in its target date funds):

Years to retirement	How much in stocks
45	90%
40	90%
35	90%
30	90%
25	90%
20	85%
15	75%
10	70%
5	60%
0	50%
5 years after	40%
10 years after	30%

The more you invest in stocks, the more risk you'll take, which means a larger payoff when the stock market does well, and also a heavier loss when the stock market does poorly. The percentages in the table are a good starting point. If you'd like to go more aggressively or more conservatively, you can increase or decrease the numbers by up to 10 percentage points. For example, about 15 years before retirement, the table says you should invest 75% in stocks. If you'd like to be more conservative, you can make it 70% or 65%. If you'd like to be more aggressive, you can make it 80% or 85%.

Having decided how much you'll invest in stocks, now you answer the second question for your asset allocation:

Among stocks, how much in international?

A good range is 20% to 40%. I picked the mid-point 30% for my portfolio. Vanguard chose 40% in its target date funds. Choose a lower number if you'd like to keep more of your investments in the U.S. Choose a higher number if you'd like to invest more outside the U.S. The exact number isn't that critical.

With the two numbers in hand, you can use them to create a 3-fund portfolio. Suppose you picked 80% in stocks and 30% of stocks in international, you'll then have this as your asset allocation:

- 56% in U.S. stocks (70% of 80%)
- 24% in international stocks (30% of 80%)
- 20% in high-quality fixed-income investments

Write these down and use them to guide you when you choose three funds for your portfolio.

Choose Investment Options in an Employer Plan

Armed with your asset allocation strategy, now you're ready to choose three funds to fill the roles in your asset allocation.

Your workplace retirement plan typically has a menu of investment options, usually mutual funds. The options vary greatly from plan to plan. Some plans have great investment options. Some plans have poor investment options. Because you have no control over the options in the plan, you can only choose the best you can among the options available to you.

To continue using our previous example, suppose this is the asset allocation strategy you came up with:

- 56% in U.S. stocks
- 24% in international stocks
- 20% in high-quality fixed-income investments

You go through the menu of investment options in your plan to find the best candidate for each category. Your plan usually has some description for what each option invests in. It usually also lists the expense ratio for each option. As a general rule, within each category, the lower the expense ratio the better.

Here's a list of funds offered by one plan I found on the Internet. Let's apply our sample asset allocation strategy and choose the investment options.

Category	Fund	Expense Ratio
Money Market	Fidelity Government Money Market Fund	0.42%
Bonds	Fidelity Long-Term Treasury Bond Index Fund	0.03%
	Loomis Sayles Core Plus Bond Fund	0.48%
	Fidelity U.S. Bond Index Fund	0.025%
	DFA Inflation Securities Portfolio	0.12%

Category	Fund	Expense Ratio
Balanced	Fidelity Puritan Fund	0.53%
U.S. Stocks	BlackRock Equity Dividend Fund	0.60%
	Fidelity 500 Index Fund	0.015%
	Fidelity Contrafund	0.73%
	Artisan Mid Cap Value Fund	0.99%
	Fidelity Low Priced Stock Fund	0.43%
	Fidelity Small Cap Discovery Fund	0.61%
	Lord Abbett Developing Growth Fund	0.69%
International Stocks	Columbia Acorn International Fund	0.99%
	Fidelity Diversified International Fund	0.75%
	Harbor International Fund	0.77%
	Fidelity International Index Fund	0.035%
	Oppenheimer Developing Markets Fund	0.83%

It's a long list but let's sift through. Remember our rule: choose index funds over actively managed funds (see page 115).

In the U.S. Stocks category, one fund has the word "index" in the name. Its expense ratio is also a magnitude lower than the expense ratio charged by other funds. Fidelity 500 Index Fund tracks the S&P 500 index, which consists of 500 large company stocks and is often used as a barometer for the U.S. stock market. We choose this fund for our U.S. stocks allocation.

In the international stocks category, one fund has the word "index" in the name. Its expense ratio is 1/20th of the expense ratio charged by other choices for this category. We choose Fidelity International Index Fund for our international stocks allocation.

In the bond category, two funds have the word "index" in their names: Fidelity Long-Term Treasury Bond Index Fund, which invests in long-term Treasury bonds, and Fidelity U.S. Bond Index Fund, which invests in more types of bonds. The latter is more broadly diversified. We choose Fidelity U.S. Bond Index Fund for our bond allocation.

When we replace the asset allocation categories with specific fund choices in this plan, our allocation then becomes:

- 56% in Fidelity 500 Index Fund
- 24% in Fidelity International Index Fund
- 20% in Fidelity U.S. Bond Index Fund

These three funds will cover both U.S. and international stock markets and high-quality bonds. The weighted average expense ratio of this mix is 0.022%, which means you pay only $22 per year for investing $100,000!

Purists will find faults with this allocation but in a 401(k) plan with only the investment options available to us, this is "good enough." When you switch jobs, you can see whether the new employer's plan has better options or whether it makes sense to roll over to an IRA (see page 83).

When you build a 3-fund portfolio on your own instead of using a target date fund, you'll also have to rebalance from time to time. We will cover that task later in this chapter on page 131.

Difference Between Index Funds and ETFs

Outside a workplace retirement plan or a 529 plan, you're not limited to a fixed menu of investment options. When you believe in the strategy of indexing over active managers (see page 115), you'll focus on buying only broadly diversified index funds and ETFs in your IRAs, HSAs, and regular taxable investment accounts. It doesn't really matter much whether you choose index funds or ETFs. I invest in a combination of index funds and ETFs in my accounts.

Like broadly diversified index funds, broadly diversified ETFs only try to match the market, without any market timing or active selection. The difference between buying index funds and buying ETFs is mostly in their availability at different investment companies. While you can buy one company's index funds at another company, it's usually more cost-effective if you buy index funds in-house (Fidelity index funds in Fidelity accounts, Vanguard index funds in Vanguard accounts, etc.). ETFs don't have that limitation. The same ETFs are available everywhere, and it doesn't cost any more when you buy Vanguard's ETFs at Vanguard, Fidelity or Charles Schwab.

Despite their narrower availability, index funds currently have an advantage over ETFs in that you can buy an exact dollar amount in an index fund but you can only buy full shares in an ETF. For example, suppose you'd like to invest $1,000. If you buy an index fund, you can buy exactly $1,000. The fund will figure out how many shares that will be, and give you say 12.179 shares. If you buy an ETF, and the price of the ETF is $168.72 per share, you can buy either 5 shares for $843.60 or 6 shares for $1,012.32, but not exactly $1,000.

Index funds also allow automatically investing fixed amounts on a preset schedule. You can fill out a form or set up online to buy $300 in an index fund on the 5th and 20th of each month. The investment company will automatically debit your linked bank account on the scheduled dates and give you index fund shares. You can't do that with ETFs unless you use a fintech startup. When you buy ETFs you'll have to place orders in real time.

Fidelity Investments recently made it possible to buy and sell ETFs in dollars in its mobile app. In the near future, I expect more companies will make it possible to place ETF orders in dollars and on automatic schedules.

ETFs have a slight tax advantage over some index funds when you hold them outside an IRA or an HSA. All else being equal, ETFs are less likely to distribute capital gains. This means you'll pay less in taxes. This is only a slight advantage because broadly diversified index funds don't distribute much in capital gains anyway. This slight advantage also doesn't exist in Vanguard ETFs over the equivalent Vanguard index funds. If the slight tax advantage is more important to you over the convenience of buying in exact dollar amounts and setting up automatic investments on preset schedules, you can decide to favor ETFs over index funds in a regular taxable account while still using index funds in IRAs and HSAs.

3-Fund Portfolio at Vanguard, Fidelity, Charles Schwab

The "big 3" investment companies Vanguard, Fidelity Investments, and Charles Schwab all offer broadly diversified index funds at very low cost. They all charge zero commission on buying and selling ETFs.

If you decide not to invest in a target date fund, here are some low-cost index funds and ETFs for building a 3-fund portfolio. You answer the same two questions on page 123:

---

1. How much in stocks?

2. Among stocks, how much in international?

You follow the same process to calculate your asset allocation percentages. After you have the portfolio in place, remember to rebalance from time to time (see page 131).

At Vanguard, using index funds:

U.S. stocks	Vanguard Total Stock Market Index Fund (VTSAX)
International Stocks	Vanguard Total International Stock Index Fund (VTIAX)
Fixed Income	Vanguard Total Bond Market Index Fund (VBTLX)

At Fidelity, using index funds:

U.S. stocks	Fidelity Total Market Index Fund (FSKAX)
International Stocks	Fidelity Total International Index Fund (FTIPX)
Fixed Income	Fidelity U.S. Bond Index Fund (FXNAX)

At Charles Schwab, using index funds:

U.S. stocks	Schwab Total Stock Market Index Fund (SWTSX)
International Stocks	Schwab International Index Fund (SWISX)
Fixed Income	Schwab U.S. Aggregate Bond Index Fund (SWAGX)

At any company, using ETFs:

U.S. stocks	Vanguard Total Stock Market ETF (VTI)
International Stocks	Vanguard Total International Stock ETF (VXUS)
Fixed Income	Vanguard Total Bond Market ETF (BND)

Rebalance

When you create a portfolio with several funds instead of using a target date fund, you're responsible for keeping your portfolio in balance. Over time, different funds will perform differently, which causes their weights in your portfolio to deviate from the percentages you originally set. You *rebalance* to put your portfolio back to the desired allocation.

Suppose you originally picked 80% in stocks and 20% in fixed-income investments. After several years, because stocks performed better than fixed income, your portfolio has become 85% in stocks and 15% in fixed income. Because you're also several years older and getting closer to retirement, if you go back to the asset allocation table on page 123, you would choose 75% in stocks now.

First you recalculate the allocation for each fund based on the new allocation. When you answer you'll invest 75% in stocks, and 30% of those stocks should be in international stocks, your new asset allocation becomes:

- 53% in U.S. stocks (70% of 75%)
- 22% in international stocks (30% of 75%)
- 25% in high-quality fixed-income investments

If you're investing on an automatic schedule, you change the split of your ongoing contributions to the new percentages. Then you sell from the funds that are overweight according to your new allocation and you use the money to buy into funds that are underweight. For example, suppose your current values and your desired values are like this:

	Current	*Desired*	*Change*
U.S. stocks	$60,000	$53,000	Sell $7,000
International stocks	$25,000	$22,000	Sell $3,000
Fixed Income	$15,000	$25,000	Buy $10,000

You calculate what it takes for you to go from the current values to the desired allocation. Then you make the trades to achieve your desired results.

Most workplace retirement plans make this process easy in the online interface. They have a procedure for changing how the ongoing contributions are allocated. They also have another procedure for reallocating existing holdings. When you rebalance in your IRA or HSA, you'll have to do the simple math and place the orders individually.

It's trickier to rebalance in a regular taxable investment account (outside workplace retirement plans, 529 plans, IRAs, and HSAs). Selling may trigger capital gains and make you pay taxes on the capital gains. Instead of selling, you can redirect any new money into your regular taxable investment account toward the lagging part of your portfolio to make it catch up.

In the previous example, you're supposed to sell stocks and buy fixed income but selling stocks in a taxable account will trigger capital gains. Instead of selling, you send all new money for this account to fixed-income investments until they catch up to the desired allocation.

It's not necessary to rebalance every year. While I still take a look every year, I rebalance only when the percentage invested in stocks deviates from my target by more than 5 percentage points. When my target is 60% invested in stocks, I'll rebalance only when my actual falls below 55% or goes above 65%. If it's still within plus or minus 5 percentage points, I do nothing.

It helps if you use software to monitor your account balances and asset allocation percentages (see page 153). You'll be able to see your current allocation quickly and decide whether it's time to rebalance.

It's still much easier when you just invest in a target date fund. In that case you won't have to worry about rebalancing at all.

Robo-Advisors

A robo-advisor, such as Betterment, Wealthfront, Fidelity Go, or Schwab Intelligent Portfolio, is an automated service for investing in other mutual funds or ETFs. They make it easy to invest exact dollar amounts into multiple funds and ETFs and to invest automatically on a preset schedule. They also take care of rebalancing.

A robo-advisor creates a set of portfolio allocations in other funds or ETFs. The service suggests an allocation after you answer some questions. You buy the suggested allocation as one basket. Using a robo-advisor gives you the same convenience of buying a target date fund. Instead of choosing a target date fund by the target year for when you'll retire, the automated service picks an allocation for you based on your answers to their questions.

Also similar to a target date fund, robo-advisor services add a layer of fees over buying the underlying funds or ETFs directly. As we saw in an example on page 119, that specific target date fund adds an overhead cost of 0.07% per year over buying the component funds directly. The fees for robo-advisors range from free to 0.5% per year above buying the equivalent funds or ETFs directly.

Some robo-advisors also perform automated trades for tax purposes. This is called *tax loss harvesting*. It's only performed in taxable accounts, not in IRAs. When the value of one fund or ETF falls below your purchase price, the robo-advisor will sell it at a loss and buy a similar fund or ETF. The realized loss can be used to offset realized gains, which lowers your taxes on realized gains. Any excess loss can be used to offset your income (up to $3,000 a year), which also lowers your taxes.

Tax loss harvesting is useful, but its effect is often oversold. It's more useful when you keep adding a large amount of new money to taxable accounts relative to the size of your existing portfolio. This is the case for new investors. After some years, as your portfolio grows in size, the new additions become relatively smaller. This makes tax loss harvesting less effective.

For example, I have some ETF shares bought 10 years ago. Even though the value of these shares may fall, it's unlikely the price will fall below my purchase price 10 years ago. As long as the price stays above my original purchase price, there is no chance to sell these shares for a tax loss. Only the new shares I bought at higher prices in recent years have a chance to fall below my purchase price and give rise to tax loss harvesting. Over time, more and more of your holdings will turn into "old shares" and become unlikely for tax loss harvesting, but the robo-advisor will still charge their fees on those shares.

I don't use a robo-advisor because I buy index funds and ETFs directly and I take on the task of rebalancing myself. I think a target date index fund works just as well in automatic rebalancing, and it costs less than a robo-advisor. When people have most of their investments in workplace retirement plans, IRAs, 529 plans, and HSAs, tax loss harvesting doesn't apply to those accounts anyway. If you're adding a significant amount of new money relative to your existing holdings in taxable accounts, automated tax loss harvesting by a robo-advisor can by valuable.

Savings Bonds

U.S. Savings Bonds are small bonds sold by the federal government to individual savers and investors. The principal and interest are guaranteed by the U.S. government. I invest in U.S. savings bonds in addition to a bond fund, because they offer a unique opportunity for individual investors in fixed-income investments.

U.S. savings bonds can be used for both short-term savings and long-term investment. Two main types of U.S. savings bonds are *I Bonds* and *EE Bonds*.

I Bonds

Series I savings bonds ("I Bonds") are linked to inflation. You get a fixed rate in effect at the time you buy the bonds, plus a variable rate that changes with inflation every six months. The fixed rate won't change as long as you hold the bonds, up to 30 years.

For example, I Bonds bought in February 2020 pay a fixed rate of 0.2% plus an inflation component of 2.02%. The inflation component will change every six months, but the fixed rate stays the same at 0.2% for as long as you keep the bonds up to 30 years. The 2.22% composite rate is comparable to the yield on an intermediate-term bond fund at this time.

Unlike other bonds whose values rise and fall inversely with interest rate movements, you'll never lose money on I Bonds. After a one-year holding period, you can redeem I Bonds for the face value plus interest at any time. In that regard, I Bonds work more like a flexible term CD. If the rates are good you can keep the I Bonds for a long time. If you see better rates elsewhere you can sell and reinvest elsewhere. You only pay a 3-month interest penalty when you redeem within 5 years.

Also unlike most other bonds whose purchasing power is eroded by inflation, I Bonds are protected from inflation changes. If inflation goes up, I Bonds will earn more. They keep up with inflation.

I Bonds are useful for both short-term savings and long-term investing. You use after-tax money to buy I Bonds but the interest earned is tax-deferred. You pay federal income tax on the interest when you sell. The interest is exempt from state income tax.

If you use I Bonds for higher education expenses when your income is under a limit, the interest is tax-free. That income limit in 2020 is $82,350 for single taxpayers and $123,550 for married filing jointly.

You buy I Bonds on the government's website TreasuryDirect (treasurydirect.gov). The bonds are issued to your account electronically. You link a bank account to your TreasuryDirect account. When you buy I Bonds, they'll debit your bank account. When you sell, they'll credit your bank account. You can buy a maximum $10,000 per year per Social Security Number, plus another $10,000 per year if you have a trust.

The fixed rate on new I Bonds being sold changes every six months on May 1 and November 1 each year. When the fixed rate is high, it's worth buying the $10,000 annual quota to lock in for the long term. I have some existing I Bonds and I'll buy more when rates are favorable.

EE Bonds

I don't own any Series EE Savings Bonds ("EE Bonds"), although they can be useful to some people.

EE Bonds being sold now work very differently than I Bonds. The current EE Bonds pay a very low rate, which is fixed for 20 years. For example, EE Bonds bought in February 2020 pay 0.1% per year, and once you buy the bonds, that rate doesn't change for 20 years.

What's the point of getting 0.1% for 20 years? You buy EE Bonds only for its special "double the value" feature. If you hold your EE Bonds for 20 years, they are guaranteed to double in value at that point. After earning practically nothing for 19 years and 11 months, in another month a $1,000 EE Bond suddenly is worth $2,000. The effective interest rate over 20 years comes out to 3.5% per year. That's a big difference than 0.1%. The 3.5% rate is much higher than the 1.9% yield on 20-year Treasury bonds at this time.

You would buy EE Bonds only if you're sure you'll hold them for 20 years. Otherwise you're better off putting the money in a savings account. If you redeem your EE Bonds before the 20-year mark, you'll get very little interest. That's like paying a huge early withdrawal penalty.

Although I don't buy EE Bonds, because I can't be sure I'll be able to hold them for 20 years, other people do just that, as an alternative to investing in 20-year Treasury bonds.

If the market interest rates go up, the advantage of the 3.5% yield from holding EE Bonds for 20 years over investing in 20-year Treasury bonds will become smaller or even negative. If market interest rates stay low for years on end, EE Bonds will shine.

The fixed rate on new EE Bonds being sold also changes every six months on May 1 and November 1 each year. Until the fixed rate goes from the current low 0.1% to above 3.5%, the "double the value" feature dominates in the value of new EE Bonds.

Like I Bonds, EE Bonds are also tax-deferred. You pay federal income tax on the interest only when you sell. The interest is exempt from state income tax. The interest is tax-free if the money is used for higher education expenses (subject to the same income limit for I Bonds).

You buy EE Bonds also on the government's website TreasuryDirect (treasurydirect.gov). The annual purchase limit is also $10,000 per Social Security Number, plus another $10,000 in a trust. The annual purchase limit for EE bonds is separate from the annual purchase limit for I Bonds. You can buy $10,000 in I Bonds and another $10,000 in EE Bonds in the same year.

CDs

I also buy Certificates of Deposit (CDs) from banks and credit unions as a part of my investment portfolio, because CDs offer a unique advantage over a bond fund. CDs are a simple but often overlooked piece in the financial toolbox. They can be used for both short-term savings and long-term investing.

CDs pay a preset interest rate for a preset term. They are very easy to understand. You know the rate and the term when you buy them. The principal and interest are guaranteed by the U.S.

government agency FDIC or NCUA. FDIC insures bank deposits; NCUA insures deposits at credit unions.

The FDIC or NCUA insurance limit is $250,000 per registration per institution. A married couple can have up to $1 million at a bank or credit union and still stay under the insurance limit:

- $250,000 in IRAs for spouse 1
- $250,000 in IRAs for spouse 2
- $500,000 in a joint account

If they'd like to invest more in CDs, they can go to another bank or credit union and invest up to another $1 million.

Direct CDs From Credit Unions

All the CDs I own were bought directly from credit unions because CDs that pay the highest rates are predominantly from credit unions. Depositaccounts.com has listings of top-rate CDs for different terms from different banks and credit unions.

You don't necessarily have to live physically close to the credit union. Some credit unions will accept you as a member if you make a one-time donation to a supported organization. All the credit unions I'm a member of are far away from me. I use online banking to purchase and redeem CDs. When you join a credit union, you must put a small amount ($5, sometimes $1) in a savings account. This is your "member share" account. When you buy CDs, you can transfer money into the member share account and then use the money in the member share account to buy CDs.

CDs have a preset maturity date. Set a calendar reminder for some days before the maturity date. The credit union will also notify you 30 days before the maturity date. You can tell the credit union what you'd like to do with the money at that time. Some credit unions take advance instructions at the time of purchase and while you're holding the CD. You can give instructions to have the money automatically deposited into the member share account when the CD matures. After the money arrives, you can then transfer the money from your member share account to wherever you want.

For short-term savings, CDs typically have a higher yield than savings accounts. The interest rate on a CD is guaranteed whereas the interest rate on a savings account can go down. The trade-off is that in case you must withdraw before the maturity date you'll pay a penalty. If the money is earmarked for an expense at a set date, you can put it in a CD. For example, if you know when you'll pay your property tax, you can put that money in a CD that will mature before the due date of the property tax bill.

For long-term investing, CDs can be a valuable addition to a bond fund. The investment world usually doesn't mention CDs at all. That's because only small retail investors can buy CDs. The $250,000 FDIC or NCUA insurance limit is meaningless to an institution investing millions or billions of dollars. There is also a misperception that only old people who are too afraid to invest put money in CDs.

To individual investors, CDs bought directly from banks and credit unions are often superior to bond funds. At least at the current time, and also in the past several years, yields of top-rate CDs have been higher than Treasury yields of the same term. For example, I recently bought a 3-year CD with a yield of 3% when the 3-year Treasury yield was only 1.6%. There are big variations in CD yields from one bank or credit union to another. With the help of the Internet, you can easily find banks and credit unions that pay top rates and avoid those that pay mediocre rates.

When you buy CDs directly from a bank or credit union, you get the valuable early withdrawal option. This option, even though not necessarily 100% iron-clad in all cases, limits your interest rate risk. If you need to withdraw early and the market interest rates have gone up, your loss is capped to the early withdrawal penalty, whereas if you sell shares in a bond fund, your loss can be more substantial.

Therefore, when you look for CDs, you should consider both the yield and the early withdrawal penalty. Choose a CD with a smaller early withdrawal penalty when two CDs offer similar rates.

Some people think you can't buy CDs in an IRA. That's also not true. Most banks and credit unions will open an IRA (Traditional or Roth) for you to buy CDs. After you fill out the transfer form, they'll contact your current IRA custodian to have a part of your IRA transferred over. When the CDs mature, you can renew the CDs to a new term, transfer the IRA to another bank or credit union to buy CDs at better rates, or transfer it back to your previous custodian.

CDs and a bond fund both have their roles. Even though top-rate CDs from credit unions look better than bond funds, you shouldn't put 100% of your fixed-income investments in CDs. When stocks fall, you'll need to sell some fixed-income investments and buy stocks to rebalance (see page 131). If all your fixed-income investments are in CDs, breaking CDs will trigger early withdrawal penalties. If you keep a bond fund in addition to CDs, it will provide liquidity for rebalancing. When you rebalance, usually you don't have to move more than 10% of your investment portfolio. If your asset allocation calls for 30% in fixed-income investments, 10% can be in a bond fund for liquidity and rebalancing while the other 20% can be in CDs.

Brokered CDs

It's also possible to buy CDs in an investment account. Banks market their CDs through the investment companies. These CDs are called *brokered CDs*. They are still FDIC-insured. Brokered CDs are more convenient because you don't have to open separate accounts with each bank and credit union individually.

I don't buy brokered CDs, because they aren't as good as CDs bought directly from credit unions. Brokered CDs don't have the early withdrawal option. If you want to get out, you'll have to sell them. If the market interest rates have gone up, you'll get a low price when you sell. Because the market for "pre-owned" brokered CDs isn't very active, you'll also face a large discount when you sell before maturity. In other words, you have both interest rate risk and poor liquidity.

Brokered CDs rarely offer a better yield than the top-rate CDs you can buy directly from a bank or credit union. When you combine the lower rate with interest rate risk and poor liquidity, it makes brokered CDs a worse deal. If you value the convenience of staying within an investment account, just use a bond fund.

Chapter 9 Stock-Based Compensation

Many employers include the employer's stock as a part of an employee's compensation package. It can take the form of stock options, restricted stock units, and an employee stock purchase plan.

Stock Options

Stock options are much less common now for rank-and-file employees, except in private startups. When you're given stock options, you have the right, but not the obligation, to buy a certain number of shares of the employer's stock at a preset price (the "strike price") when you satisfy the conditions of the agreement, typically near anniversaries of your hire date or performance reviews.

For example, if you're given options to buy 10,000 shares of the employer's stock at $1 per share, to be vested equally over four years, it means one year after you're granted the stock options, you're able to buy 2,500 shares at $1. You'll be able to buy another 2,500 shares at $1 after another year. You don't have to buy the shares right then and there but you retain the right to buy at that price.

If after four years you accumulated the right to buy 10,000 shares and by then the stock is worth $5 per share, you can buy 10,000 shares at $1 per share, sell at $5 per share, and profit $40,000. That's your bonus for working at this employer. Or you can wait and hope the share price will go to $10 per share or $50 per share someday and profit even more. If the company goes bust and the shares are worth nothing, you're not out any money but you aren't getting the bonus you were hoping for either.

Receiving a large number of stock options from a company that later becomes super-successful is a fast way to build wealth, but getting hired early into a company that later becomes super-successful requires some luck.

Restricted Stock Units (RSUs)

I never received any stock options. The company I worked for only gave Restricted Stock Units (RSUs). RSUs are like promised bonuses measured and paid in stocks.

At the time of hiring and after annual performance reviews, you may be promised a number of shares of the employer's stock to be released ("vested") over the next several years. When the promised time comes, and if you're still working for this employer, you'll receive those shares. At the time of the promise, you don't know what those shares will be worth when you receive them. If the company's share price goes up, your bonus will be larger. If the company's share price goes down, your bonus will be smaller.

For example, if you're given 1,000 RSUs to be vested equally over the next four years, you'll receive 250 shares each year. If the share price is $40 per share a year later, you'll have a bonus worth 250 * $40 = $10,000. If the share price is only $20 per share at that time, your bonus is only worth 250 * $20 = $5,000. The promise from the employer is to give you 250 shares. What those shares will be worth when you receive them depends on the stock price movements. If by the fourth year the stock price has gone up to $400 per share, your 250 shares at that time will be worth $100,000!

When you receive a $10,000 cash bonus, the employer will have to withhold taxes. You'll get a smaller amount deposited into your bank account. When you receive shares worth $10,000, the employer will also have to withhold taxes. They typically just withhold shares and give you a smaller number of shares. The promised 250 shares may become 171 shares after the employer withholds taxes. It's equivalent to giving you the cash bonus, withholding taxes, and immediately using the remaining cash to buy shares.

Because the employer is only using a cash bonus to buy shares for you, the resulting shares are nothing special. If you received a cash bonus, you could also buy the same number of shares. If the shares you buy on your own become more valuable in the future, you'll profit the same way as keeping the shares from the vested RSUs. Whether the bonus is given to you in cash or in shares isn't important. The important part is that you're given a bonus. Therefore, you would keep the shares only when you would buy shares if you were given a cash bonus.

I always sold shares from RSUs immediately after I received them, because I normally don't buy individual stocks when I have cash (see page 114). Keeping the shares from RSUs is exactly the same as using a cash bonus to speculate in the employer's stock. If I would buy individual stocks, I could speculate in other stocks as well, not just the employer's stock.

In retrospect my former employer's stock performed well. I benefited from the increase in value from RSUs that vested at a later time. I could've profited more had I kept the shares from earlier vesting but I also could've profited less if the employer's stock didn't perform well. I don't have any regret in selling the shares as my RSUs vested.

Employee Stock Purchase Plan (ESPP)

In an Employee Stock Purchase Plan, you use a percentage of your pay to purchase the employer's stock at a discount. When you participate, the employer will deduct a percentage of your pay from your paychecks and keep the money on the side. The employer will use the accumulated money to buy the employer's stock at a discount on some preset dates. How the discounted purchase price is determined varies. Many employers don't require any holding period after the shares are purchased, but some do.

My former employer has its program set to purchase the stock every six months at a 15% discount. The reference price is the lower of the price at the beginning of an "offer period" and the price at the end of a "purchase period." The offer period resets every two years. If the stock price goes down, the offer period resets immediately. This is called having a "lookback" provision, and it's very beneficial to the employees.

For example, suppose the offer period goes from May 1 of year 1 to April 30 of year 3, and the stock price at the beginning of the offer period is $20. Suppose the stock price on October 31 of year 1 is $21, and the discount is 15%. You would buy the stock at $20 * 0.85 = $17 per share. Selling the shares immediately will give you a profit of $4 per share. If the stock price at the end of the next purchase period is $18, you'll buy shares at $18 * 0.85 = $15.30 per share, giving you a profit of only $2.70 per share, but the offer period will reset and lock in this new low price of $18 per share for the next two years.

Some ESPPs don't have a lookback provision and they only discount to the price at the end of the purchase period. Some plans only offer a 5% discount instead of a 15% discount. Even at a 5% discount the return is still quite good because in a typical six-month purchase period, on average your money is tied up for only three months. Making 5% over three months is a great return.

If your employer is a publicly traded company and it offers an ESPP, consider participating at the maximum percentage of pay allowed. You're not guaranteed to make money in every purchase period but it should pay off over time.

Keeping the shares purchased from the ESPP, however, is a different story. When you already have a good profit from the discounted shares, keeping them for longer isn't worth the risk. When I participated in the ESPP, I always sold the shares immediately. The employer's stock price doing well benefited me in the value of RSUs. I didn't need to wring out every last drop by holding shares from the ESPP. If the employer did poorly, I would lose in job security, salary raises, cash bonuses, and the value of RSUs. Holding more shares would exacerbate the loss.

Chapter 10 Estate Planning

Estate planning refers to planning for what happens when you die. It's a morbid topic but things happen. Responsible people don't leave their family a mess when they die. Planning ahead of time will make your family's transition smoother, saving both time and money.

Estate planning primarily answers two questions: children and money. Who would you like to take care of your minor children if both parents die? Who will get your money if you die, and how will they get it? It's about making your wishes clear so other people won't have to guess after you die.

To most people, estate planning is quite simple. The most difficult part is having the motivation and taking the time to do it.

Will

If you have minor children, after the death of one parent, the other parent will continue taking care of the children. When you're the only parent, or when both parents die at the same time, it's not clear who will take that role. You can make your wishes clear in a *will*.

Your will doesn't have to be fancy. Nolo Press (nolo.com) sells books and software that help you prepare a will. You can find them in the public library or buy the latest from Amazon. Any simple will beats having no will. Put one in place first before you need a lawyer to prepare a more complicated will.

Beneficiaries

Who will receive the money in your workplace retirement plans and IRAs is governed by the beneficiary designation forms you put on file with the retirement plans and the financial institutions. It doesn't matter what you write in your will. The beneficiary designation on the account rules.

Whenever you switch jobs and have a new retirement plan at work and whenever you open a new IRA, make sure you fill out the beneficiary form. Set a calendar reminder to check the beneficiary designations once a year to make sure they are still current.

Joint Account and POD/TOD

If you have a joint account, the joint owner automatically gets the money when you die. Again, it doesn't matter what you write in your will. Some banks and investment companies allow you to designate Pay-On-Death (POD) or Transfer-On-Death (TOD) beneficiaries on non-retirement accounts. These designated beneficiaries will also automatically get the money after you die.

If you use POD or TOD, make sure your designations are current, just like the beneficiary designations on your retirement accounts.

Living Trust

When your accounts don't have beneficiaries or POD/TOD designations, your will takes effect. However, your will has to go through the court system. This process is called *probate*, and it can take time and cost money.

A *revocable living trust* is often used to avoid or minimize probate. If your situation is straight forward, the Nolo Press books and software can also help you create a revocable living trust.

My wife and I had an attorney create a revocable living trust for us when we had access to a group legal plan through work. It cost about $500 on top of the $200 we paid for the group legal plan. For our simple plan, any estate planning attorney would work. We transferred our home and our taxable investment accounts to the trust. When we die, the assets are still owned by the trust. A successor trustee we named in the trust will take over and distribute the assets according to the terms of the trust. Our families won't have to wait for the court. Our assets won't be consumed by the legal fees.

We don't have any kids from previous relationships. We aren't concerned about reserving money for kids after one of us dies and the surviving spouse remarries. We have no desire to release money to our families over many years versus one lump sum. Our assets are well below the threshold for estate tax ($11.58 million per person in 2020, and adjusted for inflation each year). We only wanted to use the living trust to avoid probate, speed up the process, and save on legal fees. If you have a more complicated family structure, or if you'd like to fine tune how your heirs will receive the money, or if you have enough assets to make estate tax a possible problem, consult an estate planning attorney.

Durable Power of Attorney

If you didn't die, but you're in a coma and you can't act in your full mental capacity, you'll need someone to act on your behalf. The software or the attorney who helps you prepare a will and/or a living trust will also help you prepare a *durable power of attorney*. It appoints someone to act on your behalf when you can't act for yourself.

However, in the real world, many banks and financial institutions often don't recognize the durable power of attorney that someone brings to them. They want the delegation on their own forms following their own procedures. If you can't or don't want to make the account a joint account, you should follow the financial institution's procedures to authorize another person as an agent to perform certain actions on your accounts. My wife and I have given each other this type of agent authorizations on our accounts with Fidelity and Vanguard.

Advance Medical Directive

The estate planning software or attorney can also help you prepare your *Advance Medical Directive*, also known as your living will. The Advance Medical Directive form we signed also included a Power of Attorney for Health Care Decisions.

You appoint a person as your healthcare agent to make healthcare decisions on your behalf when you aren't able to make those decisions yourself. You also specify whether you'd like receive or withhold life-support treatments in case you suffer from a terminal condition.

List of Your Accounts

If you die, will your family know where you have accounts? If they don't know, they won't be able to go get the money. Your beneficiary designations will be moot.

All it takes is a simple document listing all your accounts, and keeping the document updated as you open new accounts and close old ones. I store this document in FidSafe (see page 158).

Chapter 11 Software

Venture capitalist Marc Andreessen famously said "Software is eating the world." It's true. When we use online banking or place orders in our investment accounts, we are using software provided by the financial institutions. I also use several pieces of software on my own to manage different aspects of my finances.

Accounts and Transactions

Software can track your accounts and give you the big picture of where your money is and how your investments are allocated.

I use *Microsoft Money* to track our accounts and transactions. When everything is in Microsoft Money, I'm able to run reports and see how much we have in each account, how much we spent on what during any time period, how much our investments gained or lost, etc.

Microsoft discontinued this Windows application several years ago, but they made the last version available as a free download for everyone. You can choose either *Money Plus Sunset Deluxe* for tracking just personal accounts and transactions or *Money Plus Sunset Home and Business* if you also have a small business. The software still works on Windows 10. Although the built-in online download functionality no longer works, the user community has figured out how to make it download and import transactions from banks and investment accounts using the Quicken format. The free *PocketSense* package is able to update fund and ETF prices in Microsoft Money.

If you think it's too much trouble to tweak your computer settings and install extra add-ons, and you want an application that works out of the box, you can choose Quicken (quicken.com) or

Moneydance (moneydance.com). They have similar features as Microsoft Money. Both Quicken and Moneydance also work on Macs. Quicken uses an annual subscription pricing model. Moneydance sells for a $49 one-time purchase price plus upgrades on major releases.

If you want a free online application, you can try Money by Envestnet | Yodlee (money.yodlee.com). Instead of having you go to different accounts and download transactions yourself, the online application will download those transactions and update the balances for you automatically. You'll have to be comfortable giving the user IDs and passwords on your accounts to Yodlee for it to get authorization from your banks and investment companies.

Mint (mint.com) also works similarly. Because Yodlee's services are used by many financial institutions, they have reasons to keep the services working. I think the Yodlee online service works better than Mint.

If you only care about tracking a snapshot of the balances, not transactions within the accounts, you can just keep a spreadsheet of your accounts and update the balances manually.

Social Security Benefits

I registered an online *my Social Security* account with Social Security Administration (ssa.gov). It shows my Social Security earnings history and an estimate of my Social Security benefits. Even if you're still years away from claiming Social Security, you should create an online account with Social Security, if only to preempt identity thieves from creating an account using stolen ID information.

I use the Social Security calculator at *ssa.tools* to see how much Social Security benefits I can expect based on my earnings record and my income estimates. The benefits estimate from the Social Security Administration assumes you'll continue working at your current income until you are 62, 67, or 70. If you plan to retire or go part-time before then, the calculator at ssa.tools will show you what happens if you'll have no income or a lower income. It runs locally in the browser. Your private information doesn't go to anyone's server.

At what age you claim Social Security benefits makes a difference in the total benefits you'll receive. The earlier you claim, the lower the monthly benefits, but you'll receive the reduced benefits for more years. You need a calculator to see whether you should claim lower monthly benefits for more years or higher monthly benefits for fewer years. If you're married, when you claim also affects the benefits for your surviving spouse. When I need a recommended strategy for when I should claim my Social Security benefits, I'll use the free Social Security strategy calculator *Open Social Security* (opensocialsecurity.com). This calculator needs your Primary Insurance Amount (PIA), which is the amount of your Social Security benefits if you claim at your full retirement age. You can get your PIA from ssa.tools.

It's nice to see how the three tools work together. You use your earnings records from ssa.gov to calculate your PIA in ssa.tools, and you use your PIA from ssa.tools to calculate your optimal claiming strategy in Open Social Security.

When I ran Open Social Security, it recommended that one of us should wait until age 70 and the other can claim at any age. When we get closer to the eligible age, we will run the calculation in Open Social Security again.

Tax Returns

I always did tax returns myself. Using tax software has made it so much easier than doing it on paper forms from the Post Office. Over the years I used tax software TurboTax, H&R Block, and TaxACT. They all work. My taxes had been moderately complex with many moving parts: W-2 wages, ESPP and RSUs, self-employment, interest, dividends and capital gains, capital loss carryovers, charity donations, mortgage interest, state income tax, property tax, IRAs, HSAs, ACA health insurance and subsidies, Alternative Minimum Tax, net investment income tax, additional Medicare tax, and so on. Tax software easily handled all of them. In all these years I haven't faced anything that tax software couldn't deal with.

Nowadays I'm using H&R Block software because it's less expensive than TurboTax and TaxACT. I always use the downloaded software, not the online service, because the downloaded software is both more powerful and less expensive. The Deluxe + State version of the H&R Block software usually sells for $20-$30 on Amazon. E-filing the state return costs extra but I just print it out and mail it in. If you need to file a tax return for a trust, a partnership, or an S-Corp, H&R Block's Premium & Business version does both personal returns and business returns. It sells for $40-50 on Amazon.

If your Adjusted Gross Income is low enough (under $69,000 for 2019 tax year), the IRS offers Free File Online through a partnership with some online tax service companies. If your income is higher, but your return doesn't include self-employment, capital gains, or rental properties, United Way in partnership with H&R Block offers free filing at myfreetaxes.com. If you don't qualify for these free filing options, spending $20-$30 on downloaded tax software is still very cost-effective when going to a tax preparer can cost 10 times as much.

IRS IP PIN

Having a fraudulent tax return filed in your name has become a problem in recent years. Identity thieves create a fraudulent tax return using your name and Social Security Number and ask for refunds from the IRS. By the time you file your return, you're told the IRS already received a return under your Social Security Number.

Your tax return is then put on hold for investigation and your tax refund will be delayed.

The IRS established an Identification Protection PIN (IP PIN) program to combat this problem. When you enroll in the IP PIN program, the IRS will give you a 6-digit PIN. E-filed returns without the correct PIN will be rejected. Mailed returns without the correct PIN will be subject to extra scrutiny.

Not everyone is eligible to enroll in the IP PIN program yet. The IRS is expanding the program to more states. Currently residents in the following 19 states plus Washington, DC, are eligible to enroll in the IP PIN program:

Arizona	California	Colorado
Connecticut	Delaware	District of Columbia
Florida	Georgia	Illinois
Maryland	Michigan	Nevada
New Jersey	New Mexico	New York
North Carolina	Pennsylvania	Rhode Island
Texas	Washington	

I enrolled in the IP PIN program. The IRS sends me a new PIN every year by mail. The tax software has a place to enter the PIN. It works really well.

Password Manager

I use *KeePass Password Safe* to generate and store passwords for all my accounts. KeePass is a free open-source Windows application. It can generate long passwords with a mix of different types of characters. The passwords are encrypted and saved in a KeePass database file. You open the KeePass database file with a master password when you need to retrieve the password for an account.

Other password managers such as LastPass and Dashlane also work. I like KeePass because everything is local. The passwords are not stored online, not even in encrypted form.

Secure Document Storage

I adopted a "no paper" policy at home. I set all my accounts to receive paperless statements and tax forms. When I receive anything on paper, if it's worth keeping I'll scan it to electronic form. Otherwise I'll recycle or shred it.

I send downloaded tax forms, year-end statements, and other financial and legal documents to FidSafe. FidSafe is a free secure document storage service offered by a subsidiary of Fidelity Investments. It's also free to non-Fidelity customers. Unlike other general-purpose document storage and sharing services such as Dropbox, Box, or Google Drive, FidSafe is purpose-built for storing financial and legal documents and notes securely.

FidSafe operates like a digital safe deposit box. You can upload and download documents but there's no automatic sync between FidSafe and a local computer. Once I upload the document to FidSafe, I delete the local copy. You can pre-designate another person to access your stored documents and notes after you die. When FidSafe is notified of your death with a death certificate, that person will gain access to your documents and notes.

Chapter 12 Working with a Financial Advisor

You don't have to figure out everything on your own. If you need help, you can consult a financial advisor. You should make sure to consult a financial advisor for the right reasons and consult the right type of financial advisors.

The Right and Wrong Reasons

I'm not a financial advisor. I've never used a financial advisor. I only run a paid service that helps people find financial advisors (adviceonlyfinancial.com). In 2-1/2 years since I started the service, I helped about 300 people all over the country find financial advisors. I've seen many good reasons and some bad reasons for wanting a financial advisor.

If you want a financial advisor to help you beat the market, that's the wrong reason to use a financial advisor. Financial advisors aren't able to:

- Tell you when you should go all-in and when you should take chips off the table
- Put you in investments that will do well and switch you out of investments that will do poorly
- Tell you what's undervalued and what's overvalued
- Give you upside returns and downside protection

If a financial advisor tells you they can, run away. A financial advisor is able to:

- Help you build a roadmap after you have some significant changes in your financial life – a new job with higher income, sale of a business, when you're retiring, etc.;
- Give you a review or checkup to assess where you are and suggest what you should do;
- Serve as a second pair of eyes and help you avoid making stupid mistakes;
- Help you clean up a mess (often caused by a financial advisor of the wrong type);
- Establish a relationship to help your surviving spouse after you pass away.

If you're looking for a financial advisor to help you along these lines, you have the right reasons for working with a financial advisor.

The Right and Wrong Types

If you want a financial advisor because you just don't want to think about your finances, and you want the advisor to "just do it" for you, you likely will overpay up to 10 times more for the services. Unless money is of no object to you, you're better off working with the right type of financial advisor and pay a fair price.

Insurance Agents and Brokers

Many people call themselves financial advisors. They can be an insurance agent selling annuities and cash-value life insurance (see page 39), or they can be a broker selling investment products. When an insurance agent or a broker sells you products for commissions, they're not required to serve your best interest. They'll say their products are great for you and it's up to you to distinguish good products from bad products. Because bad products usually pay higher commissions, you're more likely to get sold bad products.

You know you're dealing with an insurance agent when the product being pitched to you has the word "annuity" or "insurance" in it. You know you're dealing with a broker when the fine print of the materials you receive have the phrase "securities offered by [so and so], member FINRA/SIPC." A financial advisor working for a broker is officially known as a Registered Representative. If you see that phrase somewhere, that's also a sign you're working with a broker. Finally, if you're not sure, just ask "Are you a broker?"

I can't say all brokers are bad advisors but the possibility of selling you products that pay the highest commissions puts you always on guard. You're never sure whether this advisor is recommending something because it's good for you or because it pays a fat commission to the advisor.

Fee-Only Advisors

Another type of financial advisors are *fee-only* advisors. The firms they work for are called Registered Investment Advisers (RIAs). They don't sell products for commissions and they only charge you fees for their services. Some advisors are *dually registered*, which means they work for both brokers and RIAs.

Fee-only advisors are required to be a *fiduciary* and serve your best interest, but serving your best interest doesn't mean charging you the lowest fees. *Fee-only* also doesn't mean charging you only a fee for advice and letting you go. Most fee-only advisors charge fees for managing investments. Their prices are usually calculated by a percentage of your assets under management (AUM). The going rate for AUM fees is 1% per year. Some RIAs charge close to 2% per year.

1% or 2% sounds small until you multiply it by the size of your investments. 1% on $500,000 is $5,000 per year, every year. 1% on $1 million is $10,000 per year, every year. As your investments grow with the market, the fees also grow. Especially for retirees with large accumulated assets, paying a percentage of investments is very expensive.

Some fee-only advisors charge a flat fee, which effectively puts a cap on the fees for assets under management. Even so, the flat fee usually still comes out to several thousand dollars a year, every year. When you're going to a financial advisor for the right reasons, your needs are more up front and episodic. After you get the advice, you should be all set. At best you need an annual checkup, which shouldn't cost thousands of dollars year after year.

Advice-Only

Fortunately, not all financial advisors sell products or manage investments. Some financial advisors charge an hourly fee or project-based fee. They don't sell any product, and they don't manage any investments. After you get the advice, you implement the advice through the online interface or customer service at the financial institutions of your choice. It's like seeing a doctor. You get the prescription, and you take the medication yourself. You do a follow-up visit when you need it. You pay for what you need, only when you need it. I call these advisors *Advice-Only* financial advisors, because they don't touch your money and they only offer advice for a fee.

Many brokers and fee-only advisors also offer to do a financial plan or a review for you. When they also sell products or manage investments, you never know whether the financial plan or review is just an opportunity for upgrading you to "full service." That's why I think you're better off going to a financial advisor who doesn't sell any product and doesn't manage any investments, period.

Unfortunately, these Advice-Only financial advisors aren't easy to find. When I went through a listing of 200 financial advisors one time, I found only two who are Advice-Only. Another time I couldn't find a single Advice-Only advisor in an entire state. Some Advice-

Only advisors are booked several months ahead for new clients. Nonetheless, if you're flexible with time and location, I think working with an Advice-Only advisor is the best way to get financial advice for a fair price.

If you'd like to find an Advice-Only financial advisor yourself, start with these organizations:

- NAPFA (napfa.org)
- Financial Planning Association (plannersearch.org)
- Garrett Planning Network (garrettplanningnetwork.com)
- XY Planning Network (xyplanningnetwork.com)

Just be aware that not all members of these organizations are Advice-Only. When I help clients find Advice-Only advisors, I go through the listings at these organizations one by one, and I screen out the ones who are not Advice-Only. I know of no shortcuts.

Appendix: Resources

You're welcome to subscribe to my blog for free updates at:

https://thefinancebuff.com/subscribe

You'll find a list of supplemental reading and calculators mentioned in this book at:

https://thefinancebuff.com/toolbox

Bogleheads (bogleheads.org/forum) is an online community of like-minded investors. I've been a member of this community since 2007. You can find me there under the user name *tfb*.

About the Author

Harry Sit is a long-time blogger at *thefinancebuff.com*. He has been sharing his personal experience and thoughts in personal finance with online readers since 2006. In 2019, 1.9 million people visited his blog.

Harry founded Advice-Only Financial, LLC in 2017 to help people find financial advisors who only give advice but don't manage investments. Since then, he has helped 300 people all over the country find such advisors.

Harry has an MBA degree in Finance. He also earned a Certified Employee Benefits Specialist (CEBS) designation from his previous work in the employee benefits field.

Harry was the author of a chapter on defined benefit pension plans in *Bogleheads' Guide to Retirement Planning* (John Wiley & Sons, 2009). His previous book *Explore TIPS: A Practical Guide to Investing in Treasury Inflation-Protected Securities* received praise from both academics and financial advisors.

Index

Made in the USA
Columbia, SC
23 February 2020